LONDON COACH HAND[BOOK]

Colin Lloyd, Jef Johnson, Keith Grimes

Capital Transport

Operators included

AWC (North Feltham)
ABBEY TRAVEL (Muswell Hill)
ABBEY EXECUTIVE TRAVEL (Barking)
ABLE (Edgware)
ACE (Tottenham)
ACEWAYS (Pentonville)
ACTON HOLIDAYS (Acton)
ALLIED (grouped with Wings)
ANDERSON (Bermondsey)
ANGEL MOTORS (Tottenham)
APPLE (Slough)
ARENA (Hersham)
ARMCHAIR (Brentford)
ARON (Northolt)
ASHFORD LUXURY inc Windsorian (Bedfont)
AVON inc Gatwick Flyer (Romford)
BANSTEAD (Banstead)
BERRYHURST (Lambeth)
BEST TOURS (Alperton)
BLUEWAYS (Battersea)
BOOKHAM COACHES (Little Bookham)
BRENTS (Watford)
BRENTON'S (Blackheath)
CABIN (Hayes)

CANTABRICA (Watford)
CAPITAL (West Drayton)
CAVALIER TOURS (Barking)
CAVALIER (West Molesey)
CENTURION (Windsor)
CHALFONT (Southall)
CHALFONT LINE (Perivale)
CHANNEL COACHWAYS (Bow)
CHIVERS (Wallington)
CLAREMONT (Worcester Park)
CLARKES (Sydenham)
COLLINS (Hanwell)
CONISTON (Bromley)
DAVID CORBEL (Edgware)
CUMFILUX (Hillingdon)
DP (Greenford)
D & J OF HARROW (Hatch End)
DAVIAN (Enfield)
DEBONAIR (Battersea)
DENNINGS (Enfield)
DIAMOND (Southall)
EBDON'S (Sidcup)
P. & J. ELLIS (Wembley Park)
EMPRESS (Cambridge Heath)

EPSOM COACHES
ESCORT (Enfield)
ESSEX COACHWAYS (Bcw)
FALCON (Shepperton)
FERNLEAF (Morden)
FINCHLEY & SOUTHGATE (New Southgate)
FIVEWAYS (Croydon)
FOREST (East Ham)
FORESTDALE (Croydon)
FRAMES RICKARDS (Bloomsbury)
GMV (Canonbury)
G & C (Queens Park)
GN (Greenford)
GAYTIME (Fulham)
GOLDENSTAND (North Acton)
GOLDEN TOURS (Shepherds Bush)
GREEN (Walthamstow)
GREY-GREEN (Stamford Hill)
GUIDELINE (Streatham Vale)
HAMILTON (Hayes End)
HAMPTON'S (Deptford)
HARDINGS (Betchworth)
HAROLD WOOD COACHES
HEARN'S (Harrow)

ISBN 185414 196 1
Second edition
Published by Capital Transport Publishing, 38 Long Elmes, Harrow Weald, Middlesex
Printed by CS Graphics, Singapore

HOUSTON & BRYANT *(Wood Green)*
HUMMINGBIRD *(Bromley)*
IMPACT *(West Ealing)*
INTERNATIONAL COACH LINES
   (Thornton Heath)
ISLEWORTH COACHES
KENTISHMEN *(Swanley)*
THE KINGS FERRY *(Gillingham)*
KNIGHTS *(Sidcup)*
LACEY'S *(East Ham)*
LEASIDE TRAVEL *(Stamford Hill)*
LEOLINE *(Chiswick)*
LEWIS *(Greenwich)*
LIMEBOURNE *(Q DRIVE)*
LINK LINE *(Harlesden)*
LOGANS *(Southfleet)*
LONDON COACHES (KENT) *(Northfleet)*
THE LONDONERS *(Nunhead)*
LONDON PULLMAN *(Ascot)*
M & M *(Harrow Weald)*
MTP *(Wanstead)*
MASON'S *(Perivale)*
MELLORS *(Harrow)*
METROBUS *(Orpington)*

MITCHAM BELLE
NAUGHTONS *(Stoneleigh)*
NEW BHARAT *(Southall)*
NOSTALGIABUS *(Merton Park)*
ON TIME *(Wandsworth)*
P & R *(Mitcham)*
PANORAMA *(Ilford)*
PEACOCK *(Tooting)*
PEMICO
PHOENIX *(Clapham)*
PRAIRIE *(Hounslow)*
PREMIER-ALBANIAN *(Watford)*
Q DRIVE *(Battersea)*
QUALITY *(Windsor)*
RALPH'S *(Langley)*
REDWING *(Camberwell)*
RELIANCE OF GRAVESEND
REPTON'S *(New Haw)*
REYNOLDS DIPLOMAT *(Bushey)*
COLIN RICH *(Wallington)*
SSS *(Euston)*
SCAN COACH COMPANY (Q DRIVE)
SEE-MORE *(East Finchley)*
SIDCUP COACHES

SILVERDALE *(North Acton)*
SILVERGRAY *(Bedfont)*
SILVERWING *(Heathrow)*
SIMMONDS *(Hayes)*
SKINNERS *(Oxted)*
SPIRIT OF LONDON *(Heston)*
STARLINE *(Watford)*
SUNBURY COACHES
SWALLOW *(Rainham)*
TWH *(Burpham)*
TELLINGS-GOLDEN MILLER *(Byfleet)*
EDWARD THOMAS *(West Ewell)*
THORPES *(North Kensington)*
TRANSYLVANIAN EXPRESS *(East Acton)*
TRAVELLERS *(Hounslow)*
TRINA TOURS *(Holborn)*
TROIKA *(Croydon)*
VENTURE *(Harrow)*
WESTBUS *(Hounslow)*
WEST KINGSDOWN *(Sevenoaks)*
WEST'S *(Woodford Bridge)*
WESTWAY *(Belmont)*
WINGS inc Allied *(Uxbridge)*
LEN WRIGHT *(Watford)*

Front cover Tony Wilson
Title page Capital Transport
Overleaf Geoff Rixon, Colin Lloyd, David Heath
Back cover Tony Wilson

Fleet lists begin on page 129

Introduction

In this second edition of the *London Coach Handbook*, we have again tried to include as many London area coach operators as we can, especially concentrating on those with interesting fleets. Although we have used the boundary of the M25 where possible, a few other coach companies have been added where vehicles may be of interest to readers. Alas, a few coach operators have ceased, a couple have been absorbed within larger groups and some omitted in this edition due to their geographical locations. We have also chosen to leave out the Green Line operations as these are to be covered in a new *London Country Bus Handbook*.

Since the 1995 edition, most companies have increased their operations, with the majority of them acquiring new or at least newer coaches. Whereas the Volvo B10M still holds the top spot in terms of new coach chassis, the Dennis Javelin, Kassbohrer Setra and Scania K113 have also made inroads in London. As for body builders, Berkhof, Caetano, EOS, Ikarus, Irizar, Jonckheere, Kassbohrer, Marcopolo, Neoplan and Van Hool have all managed to encroach on the British stronghold, Plaxton. On the midi and minicoach front, Autobus, Caetano, Cacciamali, Indcar and Robin Hood have accounted for the majority of new vehicles. As we approach the millennium, we look forward to the possibility of a world beating chassis and body combination from British manufacturers that will one day compete with the seemingly ever successful European makers.

The authors and publisher would like to thank Roy Hall, Steve Hillier, Glenn Jenkins, Keith Kiverstein, Glyn Matthews, Barry Nunn, Dennis Smith, Dave Stewart, Chris Suggitt, the London Omnibus Traction Society, the PSV Circle, all the photographers who have put themselves out to supply slides or prints at short notice and especially the majority of the operators for their assistance during the preparation of this publication. Also special thanks to Shirley Lloyd and Wendy Johnson for their patience and understanding. Where the information has been supplied by the operators, the lists contained herein are correct to September 1997.

Colin Lloyd, Jef Johnson and Keith Grimes

Abbey Travel of Muswell Hill have a fleet of five full sized coaches as well as a minibus and a minicoach. Representing the latter is J707MBC, a Toyota Coaster with Caetano Optimo II bodywork bought when four years old in 1995. It is seen near the company base in July 1997. *Keith Grimes*

A pair of integrals within the Abbey Executive Travel fleet of Barking are B534GNV, a MAN SR280H and one of the company's LAG Panoramics, 251AET. Note the two totally different liveries. Windsor coach park provides the setting for this view seen in May 1997. *David Heath*

Able of Edgware operate one full sized coach plus a pair of mini coaches. CLJ923Y is an example of the lower floored version of the LAG Galaxy design, here mounted on a DAF MB200. It was photographed on a private hire duty at the Eastbourne coach park in July 1997. *Kevin Vincent*

Ace Travel of Tottenham operate just one vehicle, this 1992 Scania K113 with Van Hool Alizee body. As can be seen, the livery is very pleasing and indeed reminiscent of that since adopted by Ralph's of Langley. It has carried its DVLA select registration from new and is seen leaving the A1M/M25 service area at South Mimms in the summer of 1996. *Colin Lloyd*

Aceways of Pentonville have two vehicles in their fleet, both full sized coaches. The newer of the pair is TIB5532, an uncommon combination of Mercedes-Benz 0303 chassis with Jonckheere Jubilee coachwork. In April 1997 it was at Sandown Park race course. *Geoff Rixon*

Since the last edition of this book, a considerable number of London operators have opted for the attractive Irizar Century body when choosing a new coach. Acton Holidays have purchased P103GHE, a tri-axle 12.37 model seen in the Atlas Road coach park in North Acton during July 1997. *Jef Johnson*

Anderson of Bermondsey operates a mixed fleet of coaches from the Autobus Classique mini coach through to full size vehicles. Representing the latter is P889BCT, the latest coach to join their fleet. It is a Kassbohrer Setra S250 Special which entered service during July 1997 in a unique livery as seen in August having crossed the River Thames and passing the Tower of London. *Colin Lloyd*

A popular purchase by several London area operators since its launch onto the UK market is the Kassbohrer Setra S250 Special. Andersons have no fewer than nine examples including P618TVL seen in Hampton Court Road during May 1997. *Geoff Rixon*

Angel Motors run a small MAN with Caetano body, in this case G948VBC on the 10.180 frame coupled with Algarve bodywork. Newer examples of this body outwardly have very little in common. *Colin Lloyd*

The clean uncomplicated lines of the ubiquitous Van Hool Alizee are depicted by N617DWY. One of a pair bought new in 1995, it was on layover in Temple Place just off the Victoria Embankment when seen in July 1996. *Kevin Vincent*

The last surviving example of a low height Plaxton Paramount with Angel Motors is this 3200 III with the optional low driving position. J864KHD has a DAF SB2305 chassis. *Geoff Rixon*

Angel Motors retain ten mini coaches among their twenty five strong fleet, the latest such vehicle is a Mercedes-Benz 611D with a coach interior built by Concept into the panel van bodywork. P699HHF was seen resting at Hampton Court Green. *Geoff Rixon*

This page top Based in Slough are Apple Coaches. Three Volvo B10Ms meet the majority of their full size coaching requirements, F881RFP being the only one of the trio with a Plaxton Paramount body, in this case a mark III version of the 3500. Sandown Park provides the setting. *Geoff Rixon*

Leaving the Hampton School while engaged on contract work is Arena of Hersham's VIB2829. This fine example of a Duple Caribbean is mounted on a Volvo B10M chassis. This original version of the Caribbean was produced for just one season before being replaced by the Caribbean II style. *Geoff Rixon*

Armchair is another company to have drastically increased the size of its coach fleet since the last edition. Although new coaches have accounted for the majority of the additions, four former Wallace Arnold examples have been bought including L916NWW, a Volvo B10M with Van Hool Alizee coachwork. It is seen leaving Millbank in March 1997 shortly after acquisition. *Colin Lloyd*

Now one of the older members of their coaching fleet, JIL3963 is one of Armchair's last four Leyland Tigers, all of which have the high floor Plaxton Paramount 3500 III design of coachwork. *Geoff Rixon*

The Dennis Javelin is now the mainstay of the Aron Coaches operation, although the coachwork has been supplied by four body manufacturers. Here in Parliament Street, L21OET shows the sole Plaxton Premiere 320 example. *Colin Lloyd*

Aron M714HBC photographed in Victoria Street when new in 1995 shows the Marcopolo Explorer introduced onto the British market that year. Mounted on the Dennis Javelin, the Portuguese built Marcopolo has found favour with a handful of London area operators. *Colin Lloyd*

Facing page
To commemorate the twenty-fifth anniversary of Ashford Luxury Coaches in 1997 P888ASH, their latest delivery, has received this silver based livery. Photographed at Richmond swimming baths, the Dennis Javelin Plaxton Premiere combination displays its livery to good effect. *Geoff Rixon*

Left Seen on a private hire at Wembley Stadium, Ashford Luxury Coaches' H588CRJ was purchased new in 1993 and features a coachbuilt Mellor body on a Mercedes-Benz 811D chassis. *Colin Lloyd*

Below left One of the relatively few Duple Lasers based in the London area is A440JJC, the only Bedford YNT in the associated Avon Coaches and Gatwick Flyer fleets, in exemplary condition for a 14 year old vehicle. *Colin Lloyd*

Below Woollons Coaches have adopted a new fleetname, AWC, and a new livery. Illustrating these to good effect is SJI5589, a Scania K112TRS with Jonckheere Jubilee P99 coachwork dating from 1986 and the only double-decker in their fleet. *Jef Johnson*

Banstead Coaches take great pride in the cleanliness and upkeep of their coaches typified by E233GPH in Cromwell Road, Kingston during March 1997. It remains one of only three Bedfords now left in stock, although most of the vehicles retain a British element with either chassis or coachwork built in the United Kingdom. *Colin Lloyd*

Banstead Coaches purchased a pair of new Berkhof Excellence 1000 L bodied Dennis Javelin coaches in 1996. Here crossing Lambeth Bridge in September 1996 is the first of the pair, N30BAN, showing the unusual italic style registration plate. *Colin Lloyd*

Berryhurst of Lambeth is one of a small number of British coach operators whose main business centres around the transportation of bands and other entertainers, mainly in Europe. From the outside, XIB5144 looks little different to any other Van Hool Astromega, but the interior is taken up with large sleeping areas to enable the passengers to fully relax between venues. Unusually, both of Berryhurst's Astromegas are left hand drive configuration as seen outside their base in May 1997. *Colin Lloyd*

Although most of the Berryhurst operations are concentrated on band usage, general coaching work and London sightseeing tours are still catered for – invariably using a trio of Caetano midi coaches. Here H8BCH crosses Putney Bridge and shows its air-conditioning pod to good effect. *Colin Lloyd*

As with Berryhurst, Best Tours of Alperton are also engaged on touring with bands and have converted all their fleet to mobile hotels. D505YPB is one of only ten Van Rooijen Odysee examples imported into Britain. There is seating for a mere sixteen with the rest of the space taken up with bunks and other luxury accessories. The distinctive angular design is seen to good effect in this view of the coach crossing Buckingham Palace Road, presumably having just completed another tour abroad. *Colin Lloyd*

Blueways of Battersea typify the medium sized London coach operator with both British and European coaches, mini through to full size. The latter type is represented here by PIB5891, an Auwaerter Neoplan Cityliner with thirty-four seats plus tables bought new in 1984, seen about to enter Parliament Square from Whitehall in May 1997. *Colin Lloyd*

Facing page The flagship of the Blueways fleet is this Irizar Century 12.37 mounted on a tri-axle Scania K113 chassis. As can be seen by the signwriting, it is the official coach of the England football team. *Geoff Rixon*

The Volvo B10M continues to be the popular choice of many coach companies despite having been in production for over a decade. Bookham Coaches TVS986 was acquired in 1989 when three years old and still looks as good as new. Note the additional roof mounted air horns and marker lights in this view as it turns towards Whitehall with a full load. *Colin Lloyd*

The only coach purchased new by Bookham Coaches is this 1994 Scania K113CRB with Van Hool Alizee H coachwork. Amid the hundreds of coaches parked at Hampton Court for the annual flower show in July 1997 is L7BKM. *Geoff Rixon*

An interesting development since the last edition witnessed Metroline acquire the Brents and Astons operations. Subsequently, the native coaching activities of Metroline have been transferred to a revitalised Brents operation, and the Astons name has been dropped. Investment in modern coaches continues, typified by N966DWJ, one of four Volvo B10Ms with Plaxton Premiere 350 high floor coachwork. *Geoff Rixon*

As well as expanding their full size fleet, Brents have also added to their midi-coaches with Autobus Classique accounting for all the additions during the last two years. New in autumn 1995, N254WDO is one of the first two Nouvelle examples to be built and has the Mercedes-Benz 814D chassis. May 1997 finds this air-conditioned midicoach crossing Lambeth Bridge. *Colin Lloyd*

21

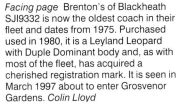

Facing page Brenton's of Blackheath SJI9332 is now the oldest coach in their fleet and dates from 1975. Purchased used in 1980, it is a Leyland Leopard with Duple Dominant body and, as with most of the fleet, has acquired a cherished registration mark. It is seen in March 1997 about to enter Grosvenor Gardens. *Colin Lloyd*

Left This Plaxton Mini-Supreme is one of a pair in use with Brentons of Blackheath. SJI9331 was purchased new in 1985. The Mini-Supreme successfully blended Plaxton styling onto the Mercedes-Benz L608D chassis cowl. It is seen on a private hire at Wembley Stadium during May 1997. *Colin Lloyd*

E635NEL is a Duple 320 bodied Dennis Javelin and is one of three such examples operated by Cabin of Hayes. May 1997 finds the vehicle in Millbank about to pass Lambeth Bridge. *Colin Lloyd*

Above Cantabrica of Watford operate an almost exclusive fleet of Berkhof Excellence bodied Volvo B10Ms. These are usually to be found on tours both in Britain and abroad. Seen here in Leeds during the Euro 96 football championships is K900CCH *Malcolm King*

Facing page – Top left Most of the full executive needs of Capital of West Drayton continue to be met by the Kassbohrer Setra. 8325MW is an S215HD Tornado type and entered the fleet in 1989. *Geoff Rixon*

Bottom left Capital have had several batches of short Volvo coaches with Plaxton bodywork of both Paramount 3200 and Premiere 320 styles. They are normally utilised on contracts associated with Heathrow and Gatwick Airports. Paramount bodied G803XLO enters Heathrow Airport. *Tony Wilson*

Top right Capital have now taken two batches of Kassbohrer Setra S250 Specials. 3401MW at Hampton Court is one of the second batch delivered in 1996. The original batch of 1995 vintage were among the first of this distinctive design imported into Britain. *Geoff Rixon*

Bottom right It was announced during the summer of 1997 that Capital was importing a number of Hispano bodied DAF SB220s for airside duties at Gatwick Airport. These were purchased from Trans Island Bus Services of Singapore and were repainted prior to use. When photographed, this vehicle was still carrying Singapore registration TIB394X prior to taking up its new duties. *Jef Johnson*

Left N588TAY, seen passing the coach station entrance at Heathrow Airport in March 1997, is the sole example of the new Iveco ECO3 chassis with Indcar 80 coachwork in the fleet of Cavalier of West Molesey. *Colin Lloyd*

Below Cavalier's latest coach is P431JDT, a relatively unusual ten metre version of the Dennis Javelin with Plaxton Premiere 320 body. *Geoff Rixon*

Facing page

Top left One of many new operators to be included in this edition is Cavalier Tours of Barking. The Camberwell premises of Redwing in April 1997 finds MIL9583, an integral Mercedes-Benz 0303 with the proprietor at the wheel. *Jef Johnson*

Top right Making their debut in this edition are Centurion of Windsor. Yet another operator who utilises European vehicles, N249NNR has Caetano Algarve II bodywork on the MAN 18.370 chassis. Full sized MAN coaches are still rather uncommon machines on British roads as depicted at Ascot Races in June 1997. *David Heath*

Bottom left Now a surprising sixteen years old, this superbly turned out Plaxton Viewmaster IV is one of the older coaches in the Chalfont Coaches fleet. With a mere thirty-six seats, SGS510W was seen in July 1997 preparing to leave the Hampton Court flower show. *Geoff Rixon*

Bottom right Chalfont Coaches have continued to purchase new vehicles since the last edition, concentrating on the erstwhile Volvo B10M with Van Hool Alizee body. M860TYC is one of four such machines purchased in 1994 which are frequently to be seen on National Express service. However, March 1997 finds this coach in Trafalgar Square passing the National Gallery on a private hire. *Colin Lloyd*

Although the majority of the Chalfont Line fleet is made up of wheelchair accessible mini coaches, the latest addition is this specially converted Van Hool Alizee bodied Volvo B10M. Having taken a year to design and build, it has been fitted with a rear nearside wheelchair lift, individual eight channel digital headphones, accessible toilet and video system. It can also be converted from C44FT to C36FT plus three wheelchairs or C24FT with eight wheelchairs. It is pictured on the Albert Embankment in May 1997. *Colin Lloyd*

Facing page Although the Caetano Optimo mark II, III and IV are a common sight on the streets of London, few of the original types are still to be seen. An exception is this 1989 example still in daily use by Chivers of Wallington. Bought used in 1992, it is still in excellent condition as can be seen in this view in Parliament Square during March 1997. *Colin Lloyd*

Another new coach type to have entered service recently is the Iveco EuroRider with Beulas Stergo E body. Channel Coachways have bought two such examples during 1996 with N12CHN seen here at the Chessington World of Adventures. The EuroRider is Iveco's first attempt at the full sized UK coach market and initial sales appear to be respectable for a newcomer to this sector. *David Heath*

Facing page Chivers acquired B545MLN from Nightingale of Langley when it was ten years old. Still looking pristine, this Plaxton Paramount 3200 bodied DAF SB2300 basks in the sun in Hampton Court Road during May 1997 just prior to receiving a new cherished registration. *Geoff Rixon*

Above left Claremont F489WPR, a Toyota Coaster with Caetano Optimo bodywork, is fitted with eighteen seats plus tables. It is seen here at the 1997 Epsom Derby Day in June. *David Heath*

Left Claremont acquired three Volvo B10Ms from Excelsior Holidays of Bournemouth in 1989. All three gained cherished plates with Excelsior, but have since been re-registered on two subsequent occasions. Despite having been photographed at Hampton School in March 1997, Claremont's D572KJT has just recently been re-registered again and now carries the cherished plate of RBZ2675. *Geoff Rixon*

Above Claremont still has a pair of the Volvo B10M's predecessor, the B58-56. Both have Plaxton Supreme IV coachwork as shown here by YGT619W leaving Millbank. *Colin Lloyd*

Facing page As one of the premier coach companies in the metropolis, Clarkes of London are rightly proud of their exceptional coach fleet. M222CLA is one of six double deck coaches in stock and one of a pair to carry Globus fleet names. Purchased new in 1995, it is a Volvo B12T with Jonckheere Monaco body and was pictured in Thorney Street coach park near Lambeth Bridge in April 1997. *Paul Stockwell*

The other four double deck coaches in the Clarkes of London fleet have yet to gain any dedicated contract livery. Introduced into the ever expanding fleet during 1997 was P77COL, seen in July 1997 at Heathrow Airport. This was one of the Clarkes coaches that made its debut at the 1997 Brighton Coach Rally. *Keith Grimes*

Clarkes have expanded substantially during the last two years and, despite massive investment in new vehicles, still retain eleven of the original design of Van Hool Alizee. Nonetheless, still looking immaculate, F673TFH coasts through Knightsbridge during September 1996. *Capital Transport*

Wisley Gardens in May 1997 finds Clarkes' P99COL, one of the newest vehicles in the fleet. It is one of seven Jonckheere Mistral bodied Volvo B10Ms now operated. The prototype Mistral for the UK market joined Clarkes during 1995 since when the design has proved to be quite a popular choice with British coach operators. *T.K. Brookes*

A surprise vehicle to join the Clarkes fleet in the summer of 1997 was this Kassbohrer Setra Special. Since 1994, the company have bought exclusively from Jonckheere but, with this demonstrator now on loan for assessment, perhaps Jonckheere's monopoly may end. St Pauls Cathedral coach park provides the setting during July 1997. *Steve Hillier*

Facing page The Plaxton Supreme coach body was introduced in 1974. Over the next eight years, six base variants were introduced, with the Viewmaster coach and Bustler bus bodies also developed from the Supreme design. Collins Coaches' UUR414W illustrates the Supreme IV style. *Geoff Rixon*

Above Volvo's initial success on the UK coach market was the B58 model. Collins Coaches still operate TGD997R, a 1977 example with Plaxton Supreme III body, as seen here with a school party cruising through Trafalgar Square in March 1997. *Colin Lloyd*

Left A511FRM at Hampton Court Road is a Jonckheere Jubilee P90 with Volvo B10M chassis. *Geoff Rixon*

35

Coniston of Bromley are another addition to these pages with their M952HRY showing the clean lines afforded to this Caetano Algarve II bodied Dennis Javelin. Bought new in 1994, it is their newest coach and is seen turning out of Parliament Square towards Whitehall and Trafalgar Square. *Colin Lloyd*

David Corbel operates a pair of these 1983 Duple Laser bodied Leyland Tigers in his fleet. Although one minicoach is in stock, most of the operation is centred on double deck coaches. Named Andy's Super Tiger, CBA1L is seen at the Chessington World of Adventures in July 1997. *Kevin Vincent*

Facing page This tri-axled Neoplan Skyliner was purchased by David Corbel during 1995 and, although new in 1984, still retains its modern appearance. A sunny Legoland at Windsor finds 620BZ during July 1997. *David Heath*

The latest member of the Cumfilux family is this relatively rare Cacciamali Ibis bodied Mercedes-Benz 814D. Registered from new with select registration N88CLC, it passes the Sir Winston Churchill statue in Parliament Square in May 1997. *Colin Lloyd*

DP Coachlines of Greenford are engaged on a London to Poland service using this Van Hool Astromega integral. One of only two vehicles in the fleet, it is seen in Buckingham Palace Road in August 1996. *Colin Lloyd*

Davian of Enfield's A61SEV is a Berkhof Esprite 350 bodied DAF MB200 new in 1984 and seen outside the company's premises in Southbury Road adjacent to the Cowie Leaside Enfield bus garage. *Colin Lloyd*

Relatively few Leyland Swifts are left operating in the London area, although one such example is depicted here retained in the fleet of Debonair of Wandsworth. G904OWY carries the Reeve Burgess Harrier style bodywork and dates from 1990. It is pictured at the company premises during July 1997. *Jef Johnson*

A handful of Hestair-Duple 425 integrals grace the fleets of several London coach operators. F365MUT is owned by Dennings of Enfield and was parked in Chase Side near Oakwood Station in July 1997. *Keith Grimes*

Dennings have a pair of Volvo B58-61 coaches on their books, one with Duple bodywork and this example with the Jonckheere Bermuda style coachwork. Purchased in 1984 when only three years old, it was captured on a private hire at Chessington coach park in July 1997. *David Heath*

Diamond operates just one vehicle, mainly on private hire work. Seen leaving Victoria Coach Station whilst on hire to Speedlink for route 777 is KIJ332, a Volvo B10M-61 with Jonckheere Jubilee body with the rear sunken saloon associated with this P90 variant.
Colin Lloyd

D & J of Harrow own just the one vehicle, a 1996 Dennis Javelin with Caetano Algarve II body. Tothill Street near New Scotland Yard finds P169ANR during July 1997 awaiting the return of its passengers from Westminster Abbey.
David Heath

41

Ebdons Tours of Sidcup have many executive coaches in their interesting fleet. Seen attending the annual Mildenhall Air Show in May 1997 is N685AHL, so far the only example of the attractive Irizar Century currently with Ebdons. *T.K. Brookes*

Among the rarest coaches ever imported into Britain is the Drogmoller. One of three bought new by Bergland of Strood during 1985 and 1986, all are now in service with Ebdons Tours. Fleet number 11 (MIW4850) is one of the two E320 Euro-Pullman examples now operated. The E330 Comet style, although similar, features a sloping window line. The Brighton Coach Rally in April 1997 finds this exceptionally fine machine parked on Madeira Drive awaiting the judges. *Chris Suggitt*

The coach park outside St Pauls Cathedral finds P & J Ellis of Wembley Park's M945JJU. It is one of a batch of three Volvo B10M-62s with Jonckheere Deauville 45 bodies bought new in 1995 and used extensively on London sightseeing duties. *Dennis Smith*

Empress of Bethnal Green has standardised on a mainly Volvo fleet since 1987 with most now carrying cherished registration marks. The majority carry Plaxton bodywork with LJI8025 typifying this trend. Clacton coach park is the setting for this Paramount 3500 III example, one of only three vehicles in the fleet to be fitted with a toilet. *Keith Grimes*

Dennis Javelins account for almost half the Epsom Coaches fleet. Obviously pleased with their initial batch bought in 1994, they have continued to purchase these locally manufactured products. Westferry in London's newly developed Docklands finds N408SPC. *Tony Wilson*

Another example of a new style of vehicle on the London scene is the Jonckheere Mistral 50. As befits one of the premier London area operators, Epsom Coaches have purchased five such vehicles including P710DPA. Pictured in Parliament Square in May 1997 when only a few weeks old, the smart lines of this new design are clearly seen. *Colin Lloyd*

As well as drastically modernising its fleet since the last publication, Escort Coaches of Enfield have also adopted a smart new livery. Shown here is TSV805, a MAN 10.180 with Berkhof Excellence 1000 Midi body dating from 1991. *Colin Lloyd*

The latest addition to the Escort Coaches fleet is this Auwaerter Transliner bodied Dennis Javelin GX300 chassis. P978HWF is a forty-nine seater with toilet, air conditioning, coffee machine and video and is pictured in May 1997 in the new Enfield Coach Park in Crown Road when only a few weeks old. *Colin Lloyd*

45

Facing page Pathfinder Coaches of Chadwell Heath has now been amalgamated into the Bow operation of Essex Coachways. Station Road in Chingford finds L970KDT, the newest one of seven Van Hool Alizee bodied Volvo B10Ms currently in use. *Colin Lloyd*

Above left KBH846V, a Leyland Leopard with Plaxton Supreme IV body new in 1980, was acquired by Falcon of Shepperton in 1986. It is seen passing the usual array of coaches along Millbank. *Colin Lloyd*

Above right Falcon Travel's only Kassbohrer Setra is TSU606, a 1985 Tornado model purchased in 1994. It is seen operating a school contract in the Hampton area during March 1997. *Geoff Rixon*

Left Fernleaf of Morden have six vehicles in their fleet. B496CBD is a Scania K112 with Jonckheere Jubilee P599 body. *Colin Lloyd*

One of the newest coaches in the Finchley and Southgate fleet is this 1987 Leyland Tiger with Plaxton Paramount 3200 III LS bodywork. This low screen example was acquired from Thamesway during 1995 having been replaced in their fleet by new vehicles for their Essex Commuter service. D588MVR was leaving the historic Hatfield House when seen in June 1997. *Colin Lloyd*

The majority of the Finchley and Southgate fleet comprises Plaxton Paramount-bodied coaches mounted on Leyland Tiger chassis. FRU675Y was acquired in 1995 from Yellow Coaches Bournemouth and was passing Trent Park at Oakwood when seen in May 1997. *Colin Lloyd*

Fiveways Travel of Croydon has four full size coaches and four mini coaches. This DAF SB3000 with Plaxton Paramount 3200 body originates from 1984 and was circumnavigating Trafalgar Square when seen in March 1997. *Colin Lloyd*

Although a minor operator compared with many in this book, Forestdale of Croydon uses this DAF engined Bova Futura integral dating from 1995. Unusually for such a small operator, it is seen here at Cardiff Bus Station working National Express route 201 to Heathrow in June 1996. *Richard Eversden*

Although Forest Coaches of East Ham have cut their fleet since 1995, Duple 425 G478SYS remains in stock . Apart from obviously attracting the racing fraternity, Royal Ascot also acts as a Mecca for coach enthusiasts by virtue of the vehicles that normally attend. *David Heath*

Several examples of the unusual Buffalo coach were built by North West Coach Sales on the Mercedes-Benz truck chassis and made their way into the London area. One example still left is Forest's H82FBY showing its distinctive lines while passing through Stratford in January 1997. *Colin Lloyd*

Facing page The latest vehicle in the Forest fleet is this Iveco ECO3 with Indcar 80 body. Photographed in April 1997 when still new, P837RYR is one of an increasing number now appearing in the London area. *David Heath*

The attractive maroon and black livery of Frames Rickards is shown to good effect in this view at Canterbury Bus Station. A13FRX is one of five Plaxton Premieres now on fleet strength, two with the Volvo B10M underframe and the remainder, as with this example, based on the Scania K113CRB chassis. *T.K. Brookes*

Below Frames Rickards are unusual in that they utilise only the Plaxton 3200 and, more recently, the Premiere 320 style of bodies. This is due to the restricted lower ground access to their premises that cannot accommodate the 3500 or 350 types. A5FRX was purchased new in 1990 and is one of a pair specially painted in British Airways Holidays contract livery. *David Heath*

Facing page G & C of Queens Park has placed this uniquely adorned Volvo B10M/Plaxton Premiere 350 into service complete with contravision windows. As far as is known, this remains the only British coach to carry such advertisements although many buses nationwide have been so treated. P233AUT was parked up in the Windsor coach park in September 1997 on a typical sightseeing tour. *David Heath*

The standard G & C livery consists of two tone blue as depicted here by P384GJM, still almost new when seen passing the Houses of Parliament. Currently the only Berkhof bodied coach in the fleet, this Axial model is mounted atop the Dennis Javelin underframe. *Colin Lloyd*

Gaytime of Fulham's J409AWF is the latest addition to this small fleet and was photographed in August 1997 at the company's parking area. It is a Volvo B10M with Van Hool Alizee bodywork and was acquired from Tellings-Golden Miller earlier in the year. *Jef Johnson*

Facing page GMV operates a mixed fleet of mini, midi and full size vehicles. GIL6096, is one of the ever decreasing number of Ford R1114 coaches left in London coupled with the uncommon shallow windowed Plaxton Supreme VI style. August 1996 finds the coach crossing Parliament Square. *Colin Lloyd*

GN Coaches of Greenford operate just two vehicles. Both are identical Volvo B10Ms with Plaxton Premiere 350 bodywork in a livery of all white. P32KWA, the newer of the pair, is seen cruising through Parliament Square during June 1997 on a typical London sightseeing tour. *Colin Lloyd*

This Caetano Algarve II coach with Volvo B10M-62 chassis represents the latest coach in use with A.Green of Walthamstow. Frequently seen on London sightseeing duties, it was caught passing Victoria Coach Station in Elizabeth Street in March 1996. *Colin Lloyd*

Still one of the most famous names on the London coach scene is that of Grey-Green. Their number 905 is one of the Van Hool Alizee examples with DAF MB230 chassis that are used extensively on both commuter services and private hire duties around London. Hatton Cross near Heathrow Airport finds the vehicle on a contract for EF Educational Tours. *Colin Lloyd*

Another facet of the Grey-Green organisation is the use of dedicated coaches on the successful Eurolines contracts linking Britain with many cities in mainland Europe. Fleet number 933 is one of eight such coaches used and, in common with all the coaches purchased since 1990, is a DAF with Van Hool Alizee body. August 1996 finds K933VCP in Elizabeth Street, Victoria, bound for foreign parts. *Colin Lloyd*

Golden Tours of Shepherds Bush have a pair of full size coaches in an otherwise all minibus fleet. Both have Dennis Javelin chassis married to the Auwaerter Transliner style of bodywork. Auwaerter are, of course, renowned as builders of the integral Neoplan range of coaches. In this view, N582AWJ stands outside Craven House at Hampton Court. *Geoff Rixon*

Goldenstand Coaches of Acton operate this LAG Galaxy bodied DAF MB200 on mainly private hire work. The only LAG in the mixed fleet, B595LJU circumnavigates the Lambeth Bridge roundabout in May 1997. *Colin Lloyd*

One of a pair of Caetano Optimo bodied Toyota Coasters in the Streatham-based Guideline fleet is 929ECH. Only recently re-registered, it is seen here passing through Wimbledon during the tennis championships in July 1997.
Keith Grimes

This attractive liveried Mercedes-Benz 0303/15 integral is the only full sized coach now left in the fleet. Acquired from Yeates as a former demonstrator in 1987, it is seen at Tattenham Corner on a sunny Derby Day. *Colin Lloyd*

Above Hamilton of Uxbridge seems to have taken a liking to less common types of coaches, such as this Leyland Tiger Doyen complete with cherished registration A6HOU as seen at Victoria Coach Station. *Colin Lloyd*

Above right Among the first UK examples of the Portuguese-built Marcopolo Explorer were the pair purchased by Hamilton in 1995. Coupled to the Dennis Javelin underframe, one assumes they must have been satisfied with their buy as a further pair arrived during 1996. M709HBC is one of the original pair, caught on National Express duties at Sheffield Interchange in September 1996. *Tony Wilson*

Right Hamilton is one of the few London coach companies to have bought new Sanos Charisma integrals. K35PLO is the only remaining example in the fleet and was found working a National Express service when seen in Oxford Street. Unusually for a large operator, no standard livery is used. *Colin Lloyd*

Above left This fine example of the Jonckheere Deauville 45 body mounted on a Volvo B10M-62 chassis belongs to Hardings of Betchworth. Purchased new in 1995, it is one of four Volvos currently in service. February 1996 found the vehicle on layover at Dorking. *David Heath*

Above right As well as purchasing new stock, Hardings have also acquired used coaches such as NSU137 from Shearings of Wigan. The high standard of presentation, coupled with the cherished registration, adequately disguises the eleven years this coach has been in service. *David Heath*

Left An arson attack at the Deptford depot of Hampton's Coaches led to the destruction of many of the fleet earlier in 1997. Fortunately, eight coaches survived including UYA699, a Volvo B10M with Duple Goldliner IV coachwork. The Goldliner was a high floor design developed from the Dominant range. *Roger Goodrum*

Broad Sanctuary with Westminster Abbey as a background provides the setting for Harold Wood Coaches B291AMG. It is one of a pair of Leyland Tigers with Plaxton Paramount 3500 II bodies and, as with all the fleet, it was purchased new. During June 1997, it received the cherished registration VJI1151. *Colin Lloyd*

To commemorate his fiftieth year in the coaching business, proprietor Fred Leach of Harold Wood Coaches has purchased this new Volvo B10M with Caetano Algarve II bodywork. Note the select registration P50HWC and the special 50th anniversary signwriting. Sadly, Mr Leach died during August 1997. *Kevin Vincent*

Facing page A recent addition to the Hearns fleet is E362NEG, a Plaxton Paramount 3200 III bodied Volvo B10M-61. Originally new to Premier Travel of Cambridge, in June 1997 it was witnessed at the Legoland coach park at Windsor awaiting the return of its load of hopefully exhausted children. *David Heath*

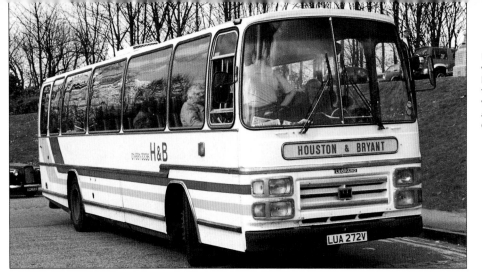

Houston & Bryant's Leyland Leopard with Plaxton Supreme IV body now holds the title of the oldest coach in the fleet. Looking rather newer than its 1980 vintage, this fine looking coach is seen at Alexandra Palace in 1996. *Capital Transport*

As with many one vehicle companies in these pages, Hummingbird of Bromley has opted for a high profile coach. This Bova Futura integral is a C49FT example of 1986 and was photographed in Birkenhead, a long way from its home base. *Glyn Matthews*

Impact of Ealing has expanded its fleet since the last book, although most of the additions have been mini and midi coaches. One exception is this less common example from the Plaxton stable, the Excalibur. Epsom Downs finds M407BLC suitably adorned with signwriting that certainly lives up to the Company name. *David Heath*

Leyland's last offering for the midi sized market was the Swift. Developed from the Roadrunner truck chassis, its brief spell of availability saw reasonable numbers sold. Impact's example is F135UMD, a Reeve Burgess Harrier bodied thirty-seven seater, seen passing Victoria Coach Station in June 1996. *Colin Lloyd*

Formerly known as Time Travel, International Coach Lines of Thornton Heath are renowned for their private hire Routemaster operations. However, they also have a coach fleet as depicted here with recently acquired N830DKU, once part of the recently defunct A & R of Bedfont fleet. It is seen at the company premises in June 1997.
International Coach Lines

Isleworth's RJI5720 is one of a pair of Plaxton Paramount 3500 III bodied Volvo B10Ms in stock seen in Parliament Square during July 1997. *Colin Lloyd*

Facing page Representing the single deck coaches in the Kentishmen fleet is this Kassbohrer Setra Rational integral of 1990. Bought by the present owner from Silver Coach Lines of Edinburgh in 1993, it is seen in Main Road in Sidcup loading up for an excursion during July 1997. *Glyn Matthews*

The Kings Ferry of Gillingham's PSU699, carrying fleet number 3.5, is a thirty-five seat Kassbohrer Setra Optimal seen crossing Victoria Street on a private hire. *Colin Lloyd*

Representing one of the 1997 intake of new Kings Ferry coaches is P661LKO numbered 5.1 in the fleet. It is a Scania K113 with Van Hool Alizee body and, as with most of the fleet, is frequently utilised on the immensely successful commuter services from Kent via the City of London to Victoria. It is seen travelling towards the Medway Towns in Victoria Street in April 1997. *Colin Lloyd*

Above Undoubtedly one of the success stories in the full size coach market over the past few years is the Irizar Century combined with the Scania chassis. There are now three basic versions of the full length model on the market, with the Midi coach now available too, albeit with a MAN instead of a Scania underframe. The most impressive is arguably the tri-axle high floor 12.37 model ably demonstrated by The Kings Ferry's 4.29 (P986LKL) at Sandown Park Racecourse. *Geoff Rixon*

Above right The Kings Ferry 3.4 (L4KFC) is a thirty-three seat MAN 11.190 bodied with the smallest available variant from the Berkhof Excellence stable, the 1000 Midi. The racecourse at Sandown Park provides the setting during April 1997. *Geoff Rixon*

Right Of the five double deck coaches with The Kings Ferry, there is only one Neoplan Skyliner. L3KFC carries fleet number 7.5 and shows the highly individual lines typical of the Auwaerter range as it crosses Lambeth Bridge in June 1997. *Colin Lloyd*

Chislehurst Road in Sidcup during July 1997 finds Knights of Sidcup's WSV486. One of a pair of Bova Futura integrals, this coach was purchased in 1991 when five years old but retains its clean modern lines. *Glyn Matthews*

Lacey's of East Ham operate a mixed fleet of full size coaches but, unusually, no mini coaches. The newest of the ten vehicles in stock is this 1989 Plaxton Paramount 3200 III bodied Volvo B10M-60 showing their uncomplicated yet pleasing livery to good effect. *Malcolm King*

Above left A major bus operator in north London, Leaside have expanded their private hire fleet of late and have also recently introduced a new livery to create a fresh image. May 1997 finds DP 1 (N551LUA), a Plaxton Premiere 350 bodied DAF SB3000, seen on the North Circular Road at Neasden. *Colin Lloyd*

Above right Leaving Edmonton Green bus station in July 1997 en route for a day's outing to Woburn Abbey is the latest vehicle to join the Leaside Travel fleet. DI 4 (P754RWU) is a high floored variant of the Hungarian built Ikarus mounted on the DAF SB3000. *Colin Lloyd*

Left Leaside Travel's TPL 1 (124CLT) is seen attending the Mildenhall Air Show in May 1997. This Leyland Tiger has the mark III version of the Plaxton Paramount 3200 bodywork, identifiable by the revised front grille and completely reshaped feature window. It originally carried a G prefix registration but has subsequently gained the plate from a former London Transport Routemaster. *T.K. Brookes*

Appearing at first glance to be another Plaxton Paramount 3500 on a Leyland Tiger chassis, Leoline Travel's RJI8032 is in fact a Leyland Royal Tiger. It is a rear engined model of spaceframe construction based upon components from the mid-engined Tiger chassis. It was caught dropping its passengers off in Hampton Court Road during March 1997. *Geoff Rixon*

Caetano of Oporto were the first continental coach builders to break into the British coach market. They continue to export many coaches to Britain some thirty years after their initial launch. Leoline's IIB8566 demonstrates the original design of the Algarve model in Sunbury Road, Hampton Court. *Geoff Rixon*

Lewis of Greenwich have made many changes to their fleet since the last publication, with many of the older coaches sold and newer examples drafted in. This particular coach is a relatively uncommon Duple Goldliner IV, the Blackpool company's attempt to combat the increasing foreign imports during the early 1980s. As can be seen in this view, it has been rebuilt with a modified grille panel disguising its appearance. Along with all the newly acquired vehicles, it now sports the new attractive livery. *Geoff Rixon*

Acquired from Thames Transit in 1995 this Leyland Tiger of Lewis of Greenwich has been extensively refurbished and fitted with a wheelchair lift. This has resulted in additional modifications having to be made to the Plaxton Paramount 3500 II body. These can be clearly discerned in this view of the resplendent PYV277 in Hampton Court coach park. *Geoff Rixon*

Although Link Line Coaches of Harlesden have previously been part of Midland Fox, London & Country, British Bus and latterly the Cowie Group, they are now independent again. This 1990 Optare StarRider midi coach bodied Mercedes-Benz 811D was acquired from Wings of Uxbridge in 1994 and within a few weeks had been re-registered to VIB7471. It is seen here outside Belgravia Police Station in Buckingham Palace Road in Victoria. *Colin Lloyd*

Below Logans Tours have a pair of scarce Van Rooijen Odysee bodied DAF coaches. This unusual yet handsome vehicle in likewise unconventional livery was seen in Trafalgar Square in May 1997, and represents one of only ten Van Rooijen Odysees to be imported and registered in Britain. *John Thompson*

Facing page London Coaches have, for many years, operated a mainly DAF/Van Hool fleet for their extensive commuter and tours fleet. During 1996, a batch of eighteen Hungarian Ikarus bodied DAFs were leased from Hughes-DAF. Having proved successful, further examples have followed during 1997. P711RWU represents one of the first batch and is seen at Hampton Court coach park in May 1997. *Geoff Rixon*

Facing page London Coaches (Kent) purchased a further sixteen DAF/Ikarus 350s during 1997 which have minor frontal differences when compared with the 1996 examples. *Colin Lloyd*

Left All the London Coaches (Kent) fleet are leased from Hughes-DAF of Cleckheaton and consequently are frequently replaced. Part of the 1996 intake of new coaches was P720RWU, a DAF with Van Hool Alizee body leaving London on a Kent bound commuter service. In May 1997, the company took over the Maidstone & District commuter services as well as Kentish Bus Green Line routes. *Colin Lloyd*

Left The latest arrivals with London Coaches (Kent) are five DAF SB3000s with the immensely popular Plaxton Premiere 350 style of coachwork built at the Plaxton factory at Scarborough. They are the only Plaxtons, and indeed the only British built coaches, in the vast London Coaches fleet. P166RWR is seen in Parliament Square in June 1997. *Colin Lloyd*

The Berkhof Excellence body is proving a popular choice among British coach operators as depicted here combined with the Dennis Javelin chassis. The Londoners have purchased eleven examples of this body style. The newest is P13LON seen cruising through Aldwych in May 1997 on its way to collect its passengers. *Colin Lloyd*

Purchased new in 1997 and seen here at Holborn, this thirty-six seater features a short Dennis Javelin with the latest Berkhof design, the Axial. Introduced as an eventual successor to the Excellence range, it is the only one of this new design currently with The Londoners. *Capital Transport*

Kuoni Tours contract livery adorns M308SHN, the sole Plaxton Premiere 350 bodied Dennis Javelin in The Londoners fleet. Having dropped its passengers at Westminster Abbey, it is seen parked in the exclusive coach bays in nearby Tothill Street. *David Heath*

Still retaining its DVLA select registration from its days with Travellers of Hounslow, H2TCC is now in service with London Pullman of Ascot. It is a Kassbohrer Setra S215HD Tornado integral and was caught in Millbank in April 1997. *Paul Stockwell*

Facing page M.C. Burcombe of Harrow Weald trades as M & M and, although only a one-vehicle operator, still manages to replace his coach on a regular basis. New in 1996 with a DVLA select plate, P66MNM is an impressively painted Scania K113CRB married to a fifty-seat Berkhof Axial body. *Geoff Rixon*

Left Mason's of Perivale's only full size coach in their nine-vehicle fleet is this Jonckheere Jubilee Deauville P599 bodied Scania K112 acquired in 1993 from Scancoaches of North Acton. TIB8563 was seen at Thorpe Park in May 1997. *Trevor Jones*

Mellor of Harrow is another company who utilises just one vehicle. When acquired in 1995 from Buddens of Romsey, the registration from the coach previously owned was transferred onto this Jonckheere Deauville P599 bodied DAF so as to retain the cherished mark. June 1997 finds the coach at the Ascot Races. *David Heath*

In recent years, Metrobus of Orpington have grown into a very sizeable bus and coach company. One of two new coaches bought in 1994 is this Dennis Javelin with Plaxton Premiere 320 body seen at Sidcup Station in February 1997. *Glyn Matthews*

Adequately showing the subtle differences between the Premiere 320 (above) and the high floored 3.5 metre 350 is Metrobus of Orpington's P214TGP. Note the higher skirt and small window above the entrance door applicable to the 350. It was seen crossing Lambeth Bridge in June 1997 heading towards Victoria. *Colin Lloyd*

Mitcham Belle have two Dennis Javelins with Duple 320 bodywork complete with cherished registrations. Both date from 1989 and were acquired from Maybury of Cranborne in Dorset during 1993. JSK957 circumnavigates Parliament Square in this view. *Colin Lloyd*

The most recent addition to the Mitcham Belle fleet is a new Plaxton Premiere 320 built on a Dennis Javelin chassis. Since the model's introduction in 1987, almost 2000 Dennis Javelins have been built. Combine this with the continued success of the Dart, and it is not surprising that the Dennis factory at Guildford now accounts for almost one third of the UK passenger carrying market. P175NAK was seen on a private hire at Worthing in June 1997 when only a few weeks old. *Jef Johnson*

The only full size coach operated by MTP of Wanstead is this Kassbohrer Setra S215HD Tornado purchased in 1991. April 1995 finds the coach crossing Parliament Square. *Colin Lloyd*

Facing page
The TAZ Dubrava was built in Zagreb, Croatia, then part of Yugoslavia. The design is based on the Mercedes-Benz O303, built under licence. Two versions were imported, the high floor D3500 and the standard height and more prolific D3200. Naughtons of Stoneleigh's example, F865ONR, represents the D3200 type and is seen here at Hampton Court in April 1997.
Geoff Rixon

Sporting a totally new style of livery for New Bharat of Southall is this Van Hool Alizee HE bodied Volvo B10M-62. The coach park at Chessington World of Adventures provides the setting in July 1997. *David Heath*

Facing page As their name suggests, Nostalgiabus of Merton Park cater for the specialised sector of the market where customers require older vehicles. KYE905 is a Bedford OB with Duple Vista bodywork and epitomises the independent operator of the late 1940s. This vehicle was new to Grey-Green in 1949 and has only recently been restored. The Stagecoach East London Leyton Garage open day in April 1997 finds this fine machine making a guest appearance. *Colin Lloyd*

KYE 905

On Time of Battersea operate a very modern fleet of vehicles. Scarce in the London area is this EOS 90 integral P897PWW. May 1997 finds this coach passing along Aldwych early on a Saturday morning en route to pick up its passengers from a central London hotel. *Colin Lloyd*

On Time have recently taken delivery of a new RH2000 bodied Mercedes-Benz midicoach built by the reincarnated Robin Hood company. P743LKL waits at Hampton Court Station in this shot taken in March 1997. *Geoff Rixon*

P & R Coaches of Mitcham have three full size coaches in their fleet including this Jonckheere Jubilee P90 bodied Volvo B10M with sunken rear saloon to seat an additional nine passengers. Purchased in 1991 when eight years old, 5398TW still retains its clean and attractive lines when seen at Aldwych in May 1997. *David Heath*

When seen at the Chessington World of Adventures in July 1997, P & R Coaches RXI4615 had still to receive full fleet livery. New in 1980, this Volvo B58 originally carried the registration HTV15V on its Supreme IV bodywork. *David Heath*

Although one of the smaller London coach operators, all three of the Panorama (Seven Kings) fleet were purchased new. This Volvo B10M shares the same body style with one of the Scanias in stock, the Plaxton Paramount 3200 III. F498RML continues to look immaculate, as borne out by this view at Chessington in July 1997. *David Heath*

Passing the side entrance of Victoria Station in Buckingham Palace Road in March 1996 is Peacocks of Tooting's DGD99T. Their fleet consists of two Volvo coaches both with Plaxton Supreme IV bodies, although this example has the B58 chassis with the newer coach having the later B10M. *Colin Lloyd*

To celebrate its twenty fifth anniversary of coach operation, Peckham based Pemico have received ten new Dennis Javelins with specially built Plaxton Excalibur bodies. They are among the first Excaliburs to be built on the Javelin chassis, and uniquely feature sunken toilets as specified by Pemico. P993NKU illustrates one of the ten currently employed during May 1997 within weeks of entering service.
Geoff Rixon

With a sizeable fleet based in Bermondsey, Pemico Travel has recently increased their fleet and indeed upped the age profile. This Autobus Classique II with Mercedes-Benz 814D chassis represents the newest midicoaches in the fleet, although a new Mercedes-Benz Vario was on order at the time of writing. Employed on sightseeing duties in Trafalgar Square is M351TDO. *Colin Lloyd*

A rare sight in London these days is the Duple Dominant II design. Although of 1980 vintage, this handy thirty-five seater is still in daily use with Phoenix of Clapham as seen passing Westminster Abbey in April 1997. *Colin Lloyd*

Quite a rarity on the London streets is this LAG Panoramic bodied DAF SB3000 wearing the distinctive livery of Phoenix. NIW5691 is seen turning into Parliament Street on sightseeing duties in June 1996. *Colin Lloyd*

Prairie of Hounslow is one of the few London coach companies to have retained a full fleet of large coaches rather than opt for mini or midi vehicles. This Jonckheere bodied Volvo B10M-61 unusually features dual nearside doorways. *Colin Lloyd*

The Bova Futura is an integral vehicle, built in Valkenswaard in Holland since 1983. Instantly recognisable by the bulbous front panel, it is produced with a choice of 3.3 and 3.5 metre height variants. Prairie's FIL7665 is the taller version and is seen cruising through Trafalgar Square. *Keith Grimes*

The coach park at Chessington finds Premier-Albanian CBM13X during July 1997. As with all the fleet except the three preserved vehicles, this Leyland Tiger with handsome Plaxton Supreme VI bodywork was purchased new by the company, in this case during 1982. *David Heath*

One of the vintage coaches is this immaculately preserved 1949 Bedford OB. As with the majority of the OBs built, this fine machine carries the Duple Vista body. A sun soaked Parliament Square finds LTA904 about to pass Westminster Abbey en route to pick up its privileged passengers. *Colin Lloyd*

Following the Q Drive takeover of the Limebourne and Scan Coach Company fleets, the latter has received an intake of new coaches. This includes P633KTF, one of the Berkhof Axial models showing the new livery to good effect. *Geoff Rixon*

Seen at Hampton Court when just a few weeks old is Limebourne's P890FMO in Trafalgar Tours livery having just completed its first eight day tour. It is one of the new Berkhof Axials introduced in 1997 following a massive investment in new rolling stock. *Geoff Rixon*

Substantial investment has seen many new vehicles enter the Q Drive fleets although older coaches have been repainted into attractive new liveries, L780GMJ is one such example, a Plaxton Premiere 320 mounted on a Dennis Javelin. *David Heath*

Some of the latest additions to the Q Drive Coaches fleet consist of a large batch of Berkhof Excellence 1000 bodied Dennis Javelins. When seen in Parliament Square in July 1996, N872XMO carried dedicated livery for Insight. *Colin Lloyd*

The highest specification coaches operated by Q Drive Coaches are afforded this smart livery of red with beige skirt and are marketed as The Glider. With a mere twenty-seven seats and toilet, they are used exclusively on tours both in Britain and abroad. P876FMO features the recently launched Berkhof Axial style coachwork as seen in May 1997 in Buckingham Palace Road. *Colin Lloyd*

A newcomer to this book is Quality Coaches of Windsor. TJI3130 is an integral Van Hool T815 Alizee and was acquired from Osborne of Tollesbury in 1996. It is seen undertaking a private hire when caught about to cross Lambeth Bridge in April 1997.
Colin Lloyd

Ralph's of Langley retain two Plaxton Paramounts, one of which, WSV468, has been repainted into this navy blue based livery for Creative Tours. Awaiting the return of its passengers from the famous changing of the guard, it was parked up opposite the Palace in Buckingham Palace Road in April 1997.
Paul Stockwell

Now with its third owner despite being only four years old, K57BAX was purchased from Shearings in 1996 having been new to Bebb of Llantwit Fardre. This Plaxton Excalibur with Volvo B10M-60 chassis shows the latest Ralph's livery of two-tone upswept stripes to good effect while on layover in Marsham Street Victoria opposite the Department of Transport in April 1997. *Paul Stockwell*

Despite a stronghold in London and the south east, the Toyota Coaster incorporating the Caetano Optimo body was a relatively uncommon sight elsewhere in Britain, although sales nationwide now seem to be increasing. Approaching Lambeth Bridge in March 1997 is the latest addition to Ralph's midi coach fleet, P773BJF. *Colin Lloyd*

Although only a year old when purchased by Redwing, L757YGE represents a batch of Volvo B10Ms bought second hand from Park of Hamilton during 1995. They were initially painted into Discovery contract livery, but have since been repainted into standard livery as depicted here at Waterloo. *Tony Wilson*

This Redwing Plaxton Premiere 350 bodied Volvo B10M-62 is one of ten coaches currently carrying Evan Evans Tours dedicated lettering that were delivered in 1996. N282OYE is seen on the Embankment in March 1997. *David Heath*

Introduced to the British market in 1995, Redwing of Camberwell has taken thirteen of these Kassbohrer Setra S250 Specials into stock. April 1997 finds P217RUU, one of the batch of seven delivered that year following the success of the earlier batch. *Colin Lloyd*

Having made its official debut at the Brighton Coach Rally in April 1997, P208RUU is only the second midicoach to be operated by Redwing of Camberwell. This Autobus Classique Nouvelle is mounted on the latest Mercedes-Benz chassis, the Vario 0.814D, and was caught at the company premises in July 1997. *Jef Johnson*

Hampton Court Green coach park provides the setting for Reliance of Gravesend's GBZ8304, the sole LAG Galaxy bodied coach in the fleet. Reliance utilise various eye-catching liveries, these being based on blue, yellow or white. *Geoff Rixon*

Reliance of Gravesend's IAZ8157 continues to operate sightseeing tours in and around London. This view, taken off Regent Street in London's West End, shows the clean lines of the Plaxton Paramount 3500 III coupled with the standard Reliance livery. *Paul Stockwell*

Portraying its DVLA select registration is Repton's P4REP. This smart blue and cream liveried Plaxton Premier 320 bodied Dennis Javelin was displayed at the Brighton Coach Rally in April 1997.
Jef Johnson

The attractive Reynolds Diplomat green, gold and white livery is displayed in this view of N4RDC at Thorpe Park in July 1997. It is a Berkhof Excellence upon yet another Dennis Javelin chassis.
David Heath

Colin Rich of Croydon has been included in this book for the first time and is represented here by NIB6829, a Volvo B10M-61 with the impressive Duple Goldliner IV body. As with the Plaxton Viewmaster, the Goldliner was introduced to try and combat foreign competition during the trend for high floor coaches in the early 1980s. It is seen at Marble Arch about to enter Oxford Street. *Colin Lloyd*

Colin Rich has a pair of Volvo B10Ms with Jonckheere Jubilee P599 coachwork and LIL7818 is the newer of the pair. Formerly in the fleet of Westway of Belmont, it has since acquired a cherished Northern Ireland registration and a new livery as shown at Southsea in July 1997. *David Heath*

Almost half of the SSS fleet consists of coaches with Scania underframes, with three embodying the K113CRB model combined with the ubiquitous Van Hool Alizee design. The fourth, N686AHL, is a K93CRB and carries the Berkhof Excellence 1000L style as illustrated here whilst attending the Euro '96 football championships in Leeds during 1996. *Malcolm King*

APA Travel Services of Euston, trading as SSS (Spanish Speaking Services), also have one vehicle carrying ISS (Italian Speaking Services) lettering. K436AVS is a rare Plaxton 425 built by Plaxton's French subsidiary Lorraine, and is seen passing the Houses of Parliament with its sightseeing party. *Colin Lloyd*

Old Steine in Brighton finds See-More Travel of Finchley's 112VMV. Very few London area based companies retain the classic AEC Reliance. This example carries the Plaxton Supreme III body and is one of three full size coaches still in daily use. *Colin Lloyd*

MFS390X was acquired in the summer of 1997 from Romney Coaches and is the latest arrival in the Sidcup Coaches operation. With Duple Dominant IV coachwork, it is a Leyland Leopard dating from 1982. It is seen on a private hire at Eastbourne coach park soon after delivery in July 1997 still carrying its former owner's livery. *Kevin Vincent*

Silverdale of Nottingham have a London subsidiary, Croxmead of North Acton. With the exception of one coach in contract livery, Croxmead coaches share a similar livery to those of their parent company as witnessed by K102UFP at Parliament Square. *Colin Lloyd*

Silvergray of Bedfont utilise their fleet exclusively for bands and other touring performers. This is reflected by the low seating capacities of their full sized coaches. C275LBH is licensed for a mere ten passengers in its role as a mobile hotel and is seen in between duties at its Bedfont depot in April 1997. *Geoff Rixon*

A new company formed since the last publication, Aviation Defence International Ground Services Ltd trade as Silverwing Services. Most of the work centres on contracts originating from Heathrow Airport. Portraying one of the four Indcar 80 bodied Iveco ECO3s is N593TAY at Hatton Cross during March 1997. *Colin Lloyd*

Simmonds of Hayes have a mainly British fleet of coaches although a trio of Volvos is operated. The Volvo B58-56 was the 11 metre model whereas the B58-61 shown here is the 12 metre version. Carrying a Duple Dominant IV body, TND131X is seen crossing Putney Bridge carrying a school party. *Colin Lloyd*

Facing page Skinners of Oxted have a fleet of twelve vehicles frequently seen on sightseeing tours in London. However, parked in the coach park in Oxford while on a private hire in March 1997 is 747SKN, a Kassbohrer Setra S250 Special integral purchased new in 1996. It is one of four coaches in the fleet to carry Europa Bus titles. *Paul Stockwell*

Spirit of London, based at Heston, now mainly undertake continental work. This Berkhof Esprite bodied Volvo B10M was one of a pair acquired in 1996 from Thamesdown subsidiary Kingston Coaches of Winterslow in Wiltshire. When caught at its home base, it had just returned from a European tour. *Jef Johnson*

Starline of Watford operate a mixed fleet from mini buses through to double deck buses as well as ten full sized coaches. Both EBZ6295 and EBZ6296 were new to Skills of Nottingham in 1983, although the latter was acquired via the Sheffield operation of Skills, which later became Don Valley. They are juxtaposed at the Walton-on-the-Naze coach park during the summer of 1996. *Keith Grimes*

Facing page Only one Jonckheere Jubilee is currently used by Sunbury Coaches, a low screen P599 model on the ubiquitous Volvo B10M underframe. HIL6754 was parked beside one of the company's Van Hool bodied Leyland Tigers when photographed. *Geoff Rixon*

Acquired from Wilson of Carnwath in Scotland in 1994 is Swallow of Rainham's DAF SB3000 with Caetano Algarve bodywork. With its passengers having spent an enjoyable day out at the Hampton Court flower show, GIL3270 pauses for the camera on 12th July 1997. *Geoff Rixon*

Although the oldest coach in the fleet of Swallow Coaches of Rainham, this 1972 Leyland Leopard was rebodied with a Willowbrook Crusader body in 1990. Displaying the uncluttered lines of its new coachwork, 8056UA was passing Westminster Abbey in Broad Sanctuary when seen returning homeward after a private hire to London. *Colin Lloyd*

Dating from 1982, Tellings-Golden Miller's DKX111X is a Volvo B10M-61 with Plaxton Supreme IV coachwork which joined the fleet during 1994. Still looking in fine condition despite being in service for fifteen years, it is seen at East Molesey in April 1997. *Geoff Rixon*

An impressive example of an executive coach is Tellings-Golden Miller's flagship vehicle, P10TGM. With seating and tables for a mere thirty-two customers, this Volvo B10M-62 with Van Hool Alizee HE body shows off its uniquely eye-catching livery at the 1997 Brighton Coach Rally. *Jef Johnson*

Three Dennis Javelins with Plaxton Premiere 320 bodies joined the Tellings-Golden Miller coach fleet in 1995 for general coaching duties. M40TGM is seen crossing Kingston Bridge in July 1996. *Geoff Rixon*

Tellings-Golden Miller provide four coaches on contract to Gullivers Travel Agency adorned in special liveries. All are Plaxton Premiere 350 bodied Volvo B10Ms with DVLA select registrations. P300GTA is seen at Victoria. *Capital Transport*

Edward Thomas & Son of Ewell has a fleet of seventeen vehicles with all but one having both British chassis and bodies. Included in the fleet are five Plaxton Paramounts, all being of the original 3200 design. This model is easily identifiable by the black ribbed panel above the headlight and grille surrounds, plus the bottom of the small feature window devoid of any visible trim. A518LPP clearly shows all these features, as seen here at East Molesey.
Geoff Rixon

Although bus work has grown somewhat since the last book, Frank Thorpe & Sons of North Kensington still maintain a substantial coach operation. Pausing at Buckingham Gate in June 1997 is TIB8571, the sole Jonckheere bodied coach in the fleet. *Colin Lloyd*

One of the most recent additions to the Thorpe's coaching fleet is K53TER, a Volvo B10M with Van Hool Alizee coachwork. It was latterly in the Cambridgeshire fleet of Kenzies of Shepreth. Seen during July 1997, it was parked in Bressenden Place in Victoria having dropped its passengers for the changing of the guard ceremony at Buckingham Palace. *David Heath*

Travellers provide luxury coaches ranging from eighteen seat Toyota Coasters through to a seventy seven seat Neoplan Skyliner. One of the former is M60TCC, an Optimo III style body from Caetano, itself partly owned by Toyota. London's Westferry on the Isle of Dogs is the location in April 1997. *Tony Wilson*

Below left The Kassbohrer Setra S250 Special has been well received by many of the larger London based coach operators. Travellers have also opted to take some, with seventeen now in stock. Ten of them have been treated to dedicated Globus livery exemplified by P137XFW at Hampton Court Palace in May 1997 a month before receiving a select TCC registration. *Geoff Rixon*

Facing page By far the highest specification coach ever ordered by Travellers of Hounslow is this Kassbohrer Setra S250 Special integral. With Mercedes-Benz V10 engine, air-conditioning, thirty-two seats with full leather upholstery, mobile telephones, walnut tables, fax machine, eight video screens and full electric central locking to mention a few of the extras fitted, it is a luxury vehicle in the truest sense. Collected personally from the Setra factory by its regular Travellers driver, it has been re-registered P200OMT and named Millennium Traveller to commemorate the forthcoming celebrations. This exceptional vehicle is seen in Bushy Park near Hampton Court in July 1997 when just a few months old. *Geoff Rixon*

Representing one of the three Travellers vehicles to carry My Bus contract livery is P222TCC. This Plaxton Premiere 350 bodied Dennis Javelin fifty-three seater is seen turning into Victoria Street in May 1997. *Colin Lloyd*

Transylvanian Express of East Acton has a Kassbohrer Setra integral coach employed on inter-European services. With its superb paint work disguising its thirteen year vintage, this S228DT Imperial example is seen leaving Victoria Coach Station in August 1996. *Colin Lloyd*

This Caetano Algarve II bodied Volvo B10M-62 is one of two vehicles delivered new in 1995 to increase the Trina Tours fleet. December 1996 finds N236NNR cruising down Victoria Street. *Colin Lloyd*

Trina Tours have increased their fleet from six to eight vehicles since the last edition with four full size coaches now in use. K420JWB is seen entering Aldwych in February 1997. *Colin Lloyd*

Troika Travel of South Norwood is represented here by the newer coach in the two vehicle operation, F823LRS. A DAF SB3000 with Van Hool Alizee body, it is seen crossing Trafalgar Square in October 1996. *Colin Lloyd*

TWH Travel of Burpham near Guildford purchased F706PAY from Redwing in 1996. This coach is one of the low height examples of the integral Mercedes-Benz 0303. The vehicle is seen looking resplendent in its newly designed fleet livery in July 1997 at Redwing's Camberwell depot. *Jef Johnson*

Venture Coaches of Harrow have a mainly Plaxton fleet made up of Supreme and Paramount models. Here is such an example, HIL5952 wearing its distinctive livery on its Paramount 3200 III body in a picturesque Hemel Hempstead whilst employed on school duties in October 1996. *Colin Lloyd*

West's of Woodford have announced that they are withdrawing from stage carriage work to concentrate solely on their coach operations. Two Caetano Algarve bodied DAFs are currently on fleet strength and, as with most of the coaches, both carry DVLA select registrations. A12BUS was on layover at Windsor coach park when seen in May 1997. *David Heath*

West Kingsdown Coach Hire has a fleet of double deck buses for several school contracts. At the other extreme, high specification Kassbohrer Setra luxury coaches are employed on excursions, tours, corporate travel and general private hire duties. The latter operation is typified at Sidcup by KWV992, one of three Kassbohrer Tornados in stock. *Glyn Matthews*

Millbank in May 1997 finds Westway's newest vehicle, N991BWJ. The only coach in the current fleet to be purchased new, it is in the new corporate fleet livery, with the previous unconventional multi-coloured examples now being repainted in this new design. *Colin Lloyd*

Westbus have revised the layout of their livery since the last edition of this book. Now looking rather different is WIB7189, one of the tri-axle Volvo B10M-53s with deck and a half Jonckheere Jubilee P95 coachwork. It was photographed on a weekend rail replacement service at Hampton Court Station in April 1997. *Geoff Rixon*

Wings Executive Travel and Allied Coachlines are associated companies based in Uxbridge. Wings tend to cater for smaller parties with their fleet of mini and midi coaches although a pair of Kassbohrer Setra Optimals are also utilised. Although of a higher specification, WET725 seen here at Hampton Court Bridge seats fewer passengers than the company's Optare StarRiders. *Geoff Rixon*

One of the London area coach companies to cater for rock band and showbusiness travel is Len Wright of Watford. K2LWB is a Plaxton Excalibur bodied Scania K113CRB converted to a mere ten-seater plus ten bunks and was pictured at the company premises in Watford in July 1997 during a break from touring. *Capital Transport*

AWC

R.D. Woollon, Falcon Estate, North Feltham Trading Estate, Central Way, North Feltham, Middlesex, TW14 6XJ

					Previous Owner
SMY633X	Leyland Tiger TRCTL11/3R	Plaxton Supreme IV	C50F	1982	Stott, Milnsbridge, 1996
RBD72Y	MAN SR280	MAN	C48FT	1982	Falcon, Shepperton, 1996
PJI4704	Leyland Tiger TRCTL11/3RZ	Caetano Algarve	C53F	1986	Coachman, Portsmouth, 1997
SJI5589	Scania K112TRS	Jonckheere Jubilee P99	CH55/19CT	1986	Gelsthorpe, Mansfield, 1996
TJI2806	Bedford YMP	Plaxton Paramount 3200 II	C41F	1986	Stringer, Pontefract, 1997
3150RU	Leyland Royal Tiger RTC	Leyland Doyen	C49FT	1987	Coachman, Portsmouth, 1997
E706GNH	Iveco 79.14	Caetano Viana	C19F	1987	McKeever & Jay, Watford, 1995
H176EJF	Toyota Coaster HDB30R	Caetano Optimo II	C18F	1991	Westbus, Hounslow, 1996

Previous Registrations:-

PJI4704	C97NNV	SJI5589	C366SVV	3150RU	D160HML
RBD72Y	RAM73Y, TVY659	TJI2806	D95ALR		

Livery:- White with yellow relief

ABBEY TRAVEL

Mandy Travel Ltd, 46 Cromwell Road, Muswell Hill, London, N10 2PD

					Previous Owner
ACH972A	Volvo B10M-61	Jonckheere Jubilee P50	C51FT	1983	Grahams, Paisley, 1985
E998DGS	Van Hool T815	Van Hool Acron	C49FT	1988	Robins, Watton-at-Stone, 1991
E57MMT	Volvo B10M-61	Plaxton Paramount 3200 III	C48FT	1988	Capital, West Drayton, 1996
E691NNH	Volvo B10M-61	Jonckheere Jubilee P50	C51FT	1988	The Londoners, Nunhead, 1995
J707MBC	Toyota Coaster HDB30R	Caetano Optimo II	C21F	1991	Armstrong, Birmingham, 1995
M525BLU	Volkswagen Caravelle	Volkswagen	M7	1994	

Named Vehicles:-   ACH972A   Westminster   E998DGS   Waltham

Previous Registration:- ACH972A   ONV650Y

Livery:- White with blue signwriting or white with red and dark blue relief.

ABBEY EXECUTIVE TRAVEL

Brian Thorogood, 13 River Road, Barking, Essex, IG11 0HE — *Previous Owner*

B534GNV	MAN SR280H	MAN	C53F	1985	Gatwick Parking, Horley, 1994
251AET	LAG G355Z	LAG Panoramic	C49FT	1986	Kinch, Barrow-upon-Soar, 1992
A8BGY	LAG G355Z	LAG Panoramic	C49FT	1989	Rowley, Emerson Park, 1994
G904WAY	DAF SB2305DHS585	Caetano Algarve	C53F	1989	Valeplain, Bilston, 1993
M808RCP	EOS E180Z	EOS 90	C49FT	1995	C & H, Rossall, 1997

Previous Registrations:- **251AET**   D24XPF   **A8BGY**   F508YNV

Livery:- Maroon with grey and white refief.

ABLE

D.H. Andrews, 83 Bransgrove Road, Edgware, Middlesex, HA8 6HZ — *Previous Owner*

CLJ923Y	DAF MB200DKFL600	LAG Galaxy	C53F	1983	Wood, Buckfastleigh, 1990
F484JBU	Citroen C25D	Citroen	M14	1989	private owner, 1991
F488JBU	Citroen C25D	Citroen	M14	1989	private owner, 1991

Livery:-.White and brown.

ACE TRAVEL

F.H. Gowen, 132 Rosebery Avenue, Northumberland Park, London, N17 9SD

K3ACE	Scania K113CRB	Van Hool Alizee HE	C49FT	1992

Livery:- White with two-tone blue relief.

ACEWAYS

M.A. Taylor & S.J. Ford, 8 Half Moon Crescent, Pentonville, London, N1 9SS — *Previous Owner*

CPT824S	Leyland Leopard PSU3E/4R	Plaxton Supreme III Express	C53F	1978	King, Dunblane, 1993
TIB5532	Mercedes-Benz 0303/15UE	Jonckheere Jubilee P50	C51FT	1982	Burton, Stanion, 1995

Previous Registration:- **TIB5532**   RAF477Y

Livery:- Various

ACTON HOLIDAYS

Acton Holidays & Travel Ltd, 356 Uxbridge Road, Acton, London, W3 9SL

M329VET	Scania K113CRB	Irizar Century 12.35	C49F	1995
P103GHE	Scania K113TRB	Irizar Century 12.37	C51FT	1997

Liveries:-   White and red (M329VET) or white and dark blue with mauve trim (P103GHE)

Named vehicles:- M329VET   London-Lviv Liner.   P103GHE   Euroliner.

ANDERSON

Anderson Travel Ltd, 178a Tower Bridge Road, Bermondsey, London, SE1 3LS   *Previous Owner*

F489YSC	Kassbohrer Setra S215HR	Kassbohrer Rational	C53F	1989	Silver Coach Lines, Edinburgh, 1997
L23CAY	MAN 11.190	Caetano Algarve II	C32FT	1994	
L61YJF	MAN 11.190	Caetano Algarve II	C35F	1994	Godson, Crossgates, 1995
L948JFU	Mercedes-Benz 410D	Autobus Classique	C16F	1994	
M568BVL	Mercedes-Benz 814D	Autobus Classique II	C25F	1994	
N415OTL	Kassbohrer Setra S250	Kassbohrer Special	C48FT	1996	
N416OTL	Kassbohrer Setra S250	Kassbohrer Special	C48FT	1996	
N115RJF	Volvo B10M-62	Jonckheere Deauville 45	C49FT	1996	
N116RJF	Volvo B10M-62	Jonckheere Deauville 45	C51FT	1996	
P618TVL	Kassbohrer Setra S250	Kassbohrer Special	C48FT	1996	
P619TVL	Kassbohrer Setra S250	Kassbohrer Special	C48FT	1996	
P789UFE	Kassbohrer Setra S250	Kassbohrer Special	C48FT	1996	
P601XFE	Kassbohrer Setra S250	Kassbohrer Special	C53F	1997	
P466YFE	Kassbohrer Setra S250	Kassbohrer Special	C53F	1997	
P467YFE	Kassbohrer Setra S250	Kassbohrer Special	C53F	1997	
P889BCT	Kassbohrer Setra S250	Kassbohrer Special	C32FT	1997	

Previous Registration:- **F489YSC**   PSU620

Named Vehicles:-

F489YSC	Helena Ria	N416OTL	Charlotte May	P601XFE	Mary Anita
N115RJF	Francesca Kate	P618TVL	Victoria Frances	P466YFE	Georgia Grace
N116RJF	Daisy Laura	P619TVL	Elisabeth Cerys	P467YFE	Kerrie Letitia
N415OTL	Emma Jane	P789UFE	Sarah Anne		

Livery:- White with green and black relief.   Special Livery:- P889BCT   Silver, light and mid green.

ANGEL MOTORS

Angel Motors (Edmonton) Ltd, Constable Crescent, Tottenham, London, N15 4QZ   *Previous Owner*

G264EHD	DAF SB2305DHS585	Van Hool Alizee H	C55F	1989	Palmer, Normanton, 1992
G896MCX	DAF SB3000DKV601	Plaxton Paramount 3500 III	C53F	1989	Shearings, 1991
G211VPX	Leyland-DAF 400	Leyland-DAF	B16F	1989	Marchwood, Totton, 1992
G948VBC	MAN 10-180	Caetano Algarve	C35F	1990	
G348VTA	Volvo B10M-60	Plaxton Paramount 3500 III	C53F	1990	Plymouth Citybus, 1993
H395CJF	Volvo B10M-60	Caetano Algarve	C53F	1990	Anderson, Bermondsey, 1994
H804EKP	Leyland-DAF 400	Crystals	C16F	1991	
J707CWT	Volvo B10M-60	Plaxton Premiere 350	C48FT	1992	Wallace Arnold, 1995
J708CWT	Volvo B10M-60	Plaxton Premiere 350	C48FT	1992	Wallace Arnold, 1995
J864KHD	DAF SB2305DHS585	Plaxton Paramount 3200 III LS	C55F	1992	
K2AME	DAF SB3000DKVF601	Caetano Algarve II	C55F	1993	
K3AME	DAF SB3000DKVF601	Caetano Algarve II	C55F	1993	
K252LGK	Leyland-DAF 400	Leyland-DAF	B16F	1993	
L932TGT	Leyland-DAF 400	Leyland-DAF	M16	1993	Capital, West Drayton, 1997
L933TGT	Leyland-DAF 400	Leyland-DAF	M16	1993	Capital, West Drayton, 1997
L951TGT	Leyland-DAF 400	Leyland-DAF	M16	1993	Capital, West Drayton, 1997
L514EHD	DAF SB2700HS585	Van Hool Alizee HE	C51FT	1994	
L515EHD	DAF SB2700HS585	Van Hool Alizee HE	C51FT	1994	
L952TGT	Leyland-DAF 300	Leyland-DAF	M14	1994	
M960GDS	LDV 400	LDV	M16	1995	
N617DWY	DAF DE33WSSB3000	Van Hool Alizee HE	C51FT	1995	
N618DWY	DAF DE33WSSB3000	Van Hool Alizee HE	C51FT	1995	
P198TWX	Mercedes-Benz 711D	Autobus Classique	C24F	1996	
P699HHF	Mercedes-Benz 611D	Concept	C24F	1996	
P187NAK	Dennis Javelin SFD731BR3TGJ4	Plaxton Premiere 350	C53F	1997	

Livery:- White with yellow and two tone blue relief.   J864KHD, K2AME, K3AME, L514EHD, L515EHD carry Golden Tours fleetnames

APPLE COACHES

Apple Coaches Ltd, Stoke Road, Slough, Berkshire, SL2 5AU   *Previous Owner*

PEG632	Bedford YMP	Plaxton Paramount 3200 II	C35F	1986	Capital, West Drayton, 1995
F171RAN	Volvo B10M-61	Ikarus Blue Danube 358	C53F	1989	
F172RAN	Volvo B10M-61	Ikarus Blue Danube 336	C53F	1989	
F881RFP	Volvo B10M-61	Plaxton Paramount 3500 III	C53F	1989	GN Coaches, Greenford, 1995
G379MAG	Mercedes-Benz 814D	Coachcraft	C21F	1989	Hardings, Betchworth, 1994

Previous Registration:- **PEG632**   C338UFP   Livery:- White with red and green signwriting.

ARENA

Arena Travel Ltd, 2 Endsleigh Gardens, Hersham, Surrey, KT12 5HE *Previous Owner*

Reg	Chassis	Body	Seating	Year	Previous Owner
DJA551T	Ford R1114	Plaxton Supreme IV	C53F	1979	Coach Services, Thetford, 1996
PJI9136	DAF MB200DKTL600	Plaxton Paramount 3500	C49FT	1983	Gardiner, Prudhoe, 1997
VIB2829	Volvo B10M-61	Duple Caribbean	C49FT	1984	Evergreen, Blackheath, 1996
C266SDL	Ford Transit	Carlyle	B16F	1985	Priory, Gosport, 1996
C886MTN	Mercedes-Benz L608D	Whittaker	C19F	1986	Paul Steed Coaches, Haverhill, 1995
MJI5037	Hestair Duple 425 SDA1513	Duple 425	C53FT	1989	Bradshaw, Alkrington, 1996
G168PUB	Toyota Coaster HBD31R	Caetano Optimo	C21F	1990	Kelly, Seacroft, 1996

Previous Registrations:-

MIJ5037 G38OHS, PBZ1397, G43YNF **VIB2829** A216YAB, JGL11, A645YOX **PJI9136** GWY981Y

Livery:- White and pink.

ARMCHAIR

Armchair Passenger Transport Company Ltd, Armchair House, Commerce Road, Brentford, Middlesex, TW8 8LZ *Previous Owner*

Reg	Chassis	Body	Seating	Year	Previous Owner
RIB4315	LAG G355Z	LAG Panoramic	C32FT	1989	MTL London Northern, 1997
RIB6197	Kassbohrer Setra S210HI	Kassbohrer Optimal	C24FT	1989	MTL London Northern, 1997
RIB6199	Kassbohrer Setra S210HI	Kassbohrer Optimal	C24FT	1989	MTL London Northern, 1997
JIL3960	Volvo B10M-46	Plaxton Paramount 3200 III	C40F	1990	
JIL3961	Volvo B10M-46	Plaxton Paramount 3200 III	C40F	1990	
JIL3962	Volvo B10M-46	Plaxton Paramount 3200 III	C40F	1990	
JIL3963	Leyland Tiger TRCL10/3ARZM	Plaxton Paramount 3500 III	C50F	1990	
JIL3964	Leyland Tiger TRCL10/3ARZM	Plaxton Paramount 3500 III	C49FT	1990	
JIL3965	Leyland Tiger TRCL10/3ARZM	Plaxton Paramount 3500 III	C50F	1990	
JIL3966	Leyland Tiger TRCL10/3ARZM	Plaxton Paramount 3500 III	C50F	1990	
K290GDT	Volvo B10M-60	Van Hool Alizee HE	C48FT	1993	
K291GDT	Volvo B10M-60	Van Hool Alizee HE	C48FT	1993	
K292GDT	Volvo B10M-60	Van Hool Alizee HE	C48FT	1993	
L916NWW	Volvo B10M-60	Van Hool Alizee HE	C48FT	1994	Wallace Arnold, 1997
L917NWW	Volvo B10M-60	Van Hool Alizee HE	C48FT	1994	Wallace Arnold, 1997
L918NWW	Volvo B10M-60	Van Hool Alizee HE	C50FT	1994	Wallace Arnold, 1997
L919NWW	Volvo B10M-60	Van Hool Alizee HE	C50FT	1994	Wallace Arnold, 1997
L116OWF	Volvo B10M-48	Van Hool Alizee HE	C28FT	1994	
L117OWF	Volvo B10M-48	Van Hool Alizee HE	C28FT	1994	
L118OWF	Toyota Coaster HZB50R	Caetano Optimo III	C18F	1994	

L119OWF	Toyota Coaster HZB50R	Caetano Optimo III	C18F	1994	
M416VYD	Volvo B10M-62	Van Hool Alizee HE	C49FT	1995	
M417VYD	Volvo B10M-62	Van Hool Alizee HE	C49FT	1995	
M418VYD	Volvo B10M-62	Van Hool Alizee HE	C49FT	1995	
N710CYC	Volvo B10M-62	Van Hool Alizee HE	C53F	1996	
N711CYC	Volvo B10M-62	Van Hool Alizee HE	C53F	1996	
N712CYC	Volvo B10M-62	Van Hool Alizee HE	C53F	1996	
N713CYC	Volvo B10M-62	Van Hool Alizee HE	C53F	1996	
P896PWW	DAF DE33WSSB3000	Plaxton Premiere 350	C53F	1997	Bibby, Ingleton, 1997

The following coaches are currently on long term hire from Hughes-DAF:-

J62GCX	DAF SB3000DKV601	Van Hool Alizee	C51FT	1992
J781KHD	DAF MB230LB615	Van Hool Alizee	C53F	1992
J831KHD	DAF MB230LT615	Van Hool Alizee	C53F	1992
J47UFL	DAF SB3000DKV601	Van Hool Alizee	C53F	1992
K529RJX	DAF MB230LTRH615	Van Hool Alizee	C53F	1993
K532RJX	DAF SB3000DKFV601	Van Hool Alizee	C51FT	1993
K537RJX	DAF MB230LTRH615	Van Hool Alizee	C51FT	1993
K106TCP	DAF MB230LTRH615	Van Hool Alizee	C51FT	1993
L526EHD	DAF MB230LTRH615	Van Hool Alizee	C51FT	1994
L528EHD	DAF SB2700DHS585	Van Hool Alizee	C51FT	1994

Previous Registrations

JIL3960	G604XMD, G401XMK	**JIL3964**	G608XMD, G406XMK	**RIB4315**	F504YNV, A17AML	
JIL3961	G605XMD, G402XMK	**JIL3965**	G609XMD, G407XMK	**RIB6197**	F81GGC	
JIL3962	G606XMD, G403XMK	**JIL3966**	G610XMD, G408XMK	**RIB6199**	F83GGC	
JIL3963	G607XMD, G404XMK					

Livery:- Orange and white   The bus fleet can be found in the *London Bus Handbook*.

ARON

Aron Coachlines Ltd, 83 Laughton Road, Northolt, Middlesex, UB5 5LW   *Previous Owner*

428EJB	Dennis Javelin 12SDA1906	Duple 320	C51F	1989	Blythin, Llandudno Junction, 1996
J308KFP	Toyota Coaster HDB30R	Caetano Optimo II	C18F	1991	private owner, 1997
L21OET	Dennis Javelin 12SDA2131	Plaxton Premiere 320	C53F	1994	
M714HBC	Dennis Javelin 12SDA2136	Marcopolo Explorer	C53F	1995	
P174ANR	Dennis Javelin SFD731BR3TGJ3	Caetano Algarve II	C51FT	1997	

Previous Registration:- **428EJB** F906UPR   Livery:- White & orange.

ASHFORD LUXURY

Ashford Luxury Coaches (Middlesex) Ltd, 373 Hatton Road, Bedfont, Middlesex, TW14 9QS
Windsorian Coaches Ltd, 103 Arthur Road, Windsor, Berkshire, SL4 1RU

Previous Owner

Ashford Luxury Fleet:-

WWL447T	AEC Reliance 6U2R	Duple Dominant II Express	C53F	1979	Heyfordian, Upper Heyford, 1993
WWL492T	AEC Reliance 6U2R	Duple Dominant II Express	C53F	1979	Heyfordian, Upper Heyford, 1993
255GPK	Dennis Javelin 11SDA1906	Duple 320	C53F	1989	
G855PJA	Ford Transit	Mellor	M16F	1990	
H745DTM	Mercedes-Benz 811D	Reeve Burgess Beaver	B33F	1990	Armchair, Brentford, 1996
H588CRJ	Mercedes-Benz 709D	Mellor	C21F	1991	
K388PJU	Dennis Javelin 12SDA2117	Plaxton Premiere 320	C53F	1993	
L227BUT	Dennis Javelin 10SDA2139	Plaxton Premiere 320	C35F	1994	
M722UWJ	Mercedes-Benz 711D	Mellor	C25F	1994	
M777ASH	Dennis Javelin 12SDA2131	Plaxton Premiere 320	C53F	1995	
P888ASH	Dennis Javelin SFD721BR3TGJ2	Plaxton Premiere 320	C53F	1997	

Windsorian Fleet:-

SSU503	Bedford YNT	Plaxton Paramount 3200	C53F	1984	
D141YMO	Bedford YMP	Plaxton Paramount 3200 III	C35F	1987	
E509JWP	Dennis Javelin 12SDA1908	Plaxton Paramount 3200 III	C49FT	1988	
F355DVR	Mercedes-Benz 609D	Mellor	C21F	1989	Ashford Luxury, Bedfont, 1995
G250CPS	Dennis Javelin 11SDA1906	Plaxton Paramount 3200 III	C53F	1989	Jamieson, Cullivoe, Shetland Islands, 1997
H166EJU	Dennis Javelin 11SDA1906	Duple 320	C53F	1991	
M887WAK	Dennis Javelin 12SDA2131	Plaxton Premiere 320	C49FT	1995	Ashford Luxury, Bedfont, 1995
N222ASH	Mercedes-Benz 811D	Mellor	C25F	1996	
N333ASH	Dennis Javelin 12SDA2155	Plaxton Premiere 320	C53F	1996	

Previous Registrations:-

255GPK	F311URU		**WWL447T**	YPL66T, 9467MU, HIL7403	**WWL492T**	YPL99T, 9682FH
SSU503	A511CAN				

Livery:- White with two tone blue relief.
WWL447T & WWL492T carry Feltham Aviation fleetnames. P888ASH is silver with two-tone blue relief (25th Anniversary).

AVON/GATWICK FLYER

G.C. & C.A. Tovey & R.M. Seboa, 90 North Street, Romford, Essex, RM1 1DA
Gatwick Flyer Ltd, 90 North Street, Romford, Essex, RM1 1DA

Previous Owner

3	J135OBU	Peugeot-Talbot Express	Made To Measure	M15	1992	
5	G236HKY	Citroen C25D	Crystals	M15	1989	
6	E671DPD	Mercedes-Benz 609D	Crystals	C26F	1988	
10	SIB7517	DAF MB200DKFL600	Berkhof Esprite 350	C53F	1984	Chartercoach, Dovercourt, 1992
11	VFJ586	DAF MB200DKFL600	Berkhof Esprite 350	C49FT	1984	Dereham Coaches, 1992
12	A440JJC	Bedford YNT	Duple Laser	C53F	1983	Young, Romford, 1992
13	A502SGS	Bedford SB5	Wright TT	B51F	1984	London Borough of Havering, 1992
14	F183LVU	Mazda E2200	Made To Measure	M14	1989	
16	K858EWF	Leyland-DAF 400	Autobus Classique	M16	1993	
19	C91WCJ	Mercedes-Benz L608D	Reeve Burgess	C19F	1985	Ipswich Travel, 1991
	ULS674T	Leyland Fleetline FE30AGR	Eastern Coach Works	H43/32F	1979	Brentwood Coaches, Little Waltham, 1996
	YSU986	Scania K112CRS	Berkhof Esprite 340	C53F	1985	The Londoners, Nunhead, 1993
	C708HWC	DAF MB200DKFL600	Berkhof Esprite 340	C53F	1985	London Buses, 1993
	G469JNH	DAFSB2305DHS585	Jonckheere Deauville P599	C51FT	1990	Luckett, Fareham, 1995
	G851LHE	Citroen C25D	Crystals	M13	1990	
	J270NNC	Scania K93CRB	Plaxton Premiere 320	C53F	1992	Shearings, 1997
	J284NNC	Scania K93CRB	Plaxton Premiere 320	C53F	1992	Shearings, 1997
	M146ROL	Ford Transit	Ford	M8	1994	BT, 1997
	N129CMT	Ford Transit	Ford	M11	1996	
	N138CMT	Ford Transit	Ford	M11	1996	
	N158MGO	Mercedes-Benz 711D	Crystals	C23F	1996	
	N435NGF	Mercedes-Benz 711D	Crystals	C23F	1996	
	N436NGF	Mercedes-Benz 711D	Crystals	C23F	1996	

Previous Registrations:-

VFJ586 A169OHJ   **SIB7517** B593XNO   **YSU986** B414DHK

Liveries:-   Avon:- White with multicoloured fleetnames.
            Gatwick Flyer:- White with maroon signwriting.

BANSTEAD

Banstead Coaches Ltd, 1 Shrubland Road, Banstead, Surrey, SM7 2ES

					Previous Owner
TPJ272S	Bedford YMT	Van Hool McArdle 300	C53F	1977	
D72HRU	Bedford Venturer YNV	Plaxton Paramount 3200 III	C53F	1987	
E466DMY	Freight-Rover Sherpa	Crystals	C16F	1988	Marksman, Gatwick, 1991
E233GPH	Bedford Venturer YNV	Plaxton Paramount 3200 III	C55F	1988	
E167TWO	Freight-Rover Sherpa	Carlyle Citybus 2	B20F	1988	National Welsh, 1995
F864HGX	Peugeot-Talbot Express	Crystals	M14	1988	
G951WNR	Dennis Javelin 11SDA1906	Plaxton Paramount 3200 III	C53F	1989	
G952WNR	Dennis Javelin 12SDA1907	Plaxton Paramount 3200 III	C55F	1989	
G433YAY	Dennis Javelin 12SDA1907	Plaxton Paramount 3200 III	C55F	1990	
H722VWU	Scania K93CRB	Plaxton Paramount 3500 III	C53F	1991	Dodsworth, Boroughbridge, 1993
L164PDT	Dennis Javelin 12SDA2131	Plaxton Premiere 320	C53F	1994	
M427WAK	Dennis Javelin 12SDA2131	Plaxton Premiere 320	C53F	1995	
N30BAN	Dennis Javelin 12SDA2136	Berkhof Excellence 1000L	C53F	1996	
P4BAN	Dennis Javelin SFD721BR3TGJ3	Berkhof Excellence 1000L	C53F	1996	

Livery:- White with pink relief.

BERRYHURST

Domino Finance Ltd, Keltan House, 1 Sail Street, Lambeth, London, SE11 6NQ

					Previous Owner
331BCH	Van Hool TD824	Van Hool Astromega	CH5/11FT	?	unknown operator, Belgium, 1995
XIB5144	Van Hool TD824	Van Hool Astromega	CH5/11FT	?	unknown operator, Belgium, 1995
MUJ208	Volvo B10M-53	Berkhof Emperor 395	CH5/13FT	1985	The Kings Ferry, Gillingham, 1992
MIB644	Scania K112TRS	Berkhof Emperor 395	CH5/11CT	1986	The Kings Ferry, Gillingham, 1991
MIB642	Scania K112TRS	Berkhof Emperor 395	CH5/11CT	1986	The Kings Ferry, Gillingham, 1991
NIL2546	LAG G355Z	LAG Panoramic	C30FT	1987	
NIL2544	DAF SBR3000DKZ570	Plaxton Paramount 4000 II	CH5/11CT	1988	Park, Hamilton, 1992
NIL2545	DAF SBR3000DKZ570	Plaxton Paramount 4000 II	CH5/11CT	1988	Park, Hamilton, 1992
NIL2542	DAF SB3000DKV601	Van Hool Alizee H	C20FT	1988	
NIL2543	DAF SB3000DKV601	Van Hool Alizee H	C20FT	1988	
H8BCH	MAN 16.280	Caetano Algarve	C29FT	1991	
J7BCH	Toyota Coaster HDB30R	Caetano Optimo II	C18F	1991	
J9BCH	Toyota Coaster HDB30R	Caetano Optimo II	C21F	1991	

Note:- 331BCH and XIB5144 are left hand drive vehicles.

With the exception of the three midi coaches and NIL2546, all vehicles are generally employed on touring with bands, usually abroad.
Hence, they are fitted with bunks as follows:-
12 bunks:- MUJ208, NIL2542, NIL2543   15 bunks:- MIB642 and MIB644   16 bunks:- 331BCH, XIB5144, NIL2544, NIL2545

331BCH	VV 60 HZ	(Belgium)	**NIL2542**	E657KCX		**NIL2545**	E311AGA
MIB642	C691KVW		**NIL2543**	E658KCX		**NIL2546**	D731BPF
MIB644	C589KTW		**NIL2544**	E309AGA		**XIB5144**	? (Belgium), J62DYR
MUJ208	B571AVW						

Livery:- Silver and blue or white with blue signwriting.

BEST TOURS

Javaward Ltd, 10 Priory Gardens, Alperton, London, W5 1DX

D505YPB	DAF SB2300DHS585	Van Rooijen Odysee	C16FT	1986
F765XNH	LAG G355Z	LAG Panoramic	C16FT	1989
G991FVV	LAG G355Z	LAG Panoramic	C16FT	1989

Named Vehicles:- D505YPB Global Rock n' Roller   F765XNH Globestar   G991FVV Globehopper

Livery:- Dark metallic blue and white or two tone blue and white.

BLUEWAYS

Blueways Coaches Ltd, 49 Winders Road, Battersea, London, SW11 3HE   *Previous Owner*

PIB5268	Mercedes-Benz L608D	Whittaker	C21F	1983	Park Avenue, Allerton Bywater, 1989
PIB5891	Auwaerter Neoplan N116	Auwaerter Cityliner	C34FT	1984	
HIL5680	Mercedes-Benz 0303/15R	Mercedes-Benz	C49FT	1986	Team Travel, Horsforth, 1996
F634GAK	Mercedes-Benz 811D	Reeve Burgess Beaver	C25F	1989	
P26RGO	Scania K113TRB	Irizar Century 12.37	C38FT	1996	

Previous Registrations:-

HIL5680	C647VNR, GBH83, C751MWE	**PIB5268**	A757WHL	**PIB5891** A344UFE

Livery:- Metallic blue and white or two tone blue with red relief.

Special Livery:- P26RGO is white with blue, green and orange relief and carries logos for Green Flag Team England soccer squad.

BOOKHAM COACHES

R.J. O'Reilly & C.A. King, Challacot, Guildford Road, Little Bookham, Surrey, KT23 4HB

					Previous Owner
MGC337V	Leyland Leopard PSU5C/4R	Plaxton Supreme IV	C50F	1979	Epsom Coaches, 1993
GVS385	Volvo B10M-61	Van Hool Alizee H	C57F	1985	Sworder, Walkern, 1989
TSV758	Scania K112CRS	Van Hool Alizee H	C53F	1986	BCP, Gatwick, 1988
TVS986	Volvo B10M-61	Van Hool Alizee H	C53F	1986	Sworder, Walkern, 1989
J212SPA	Kassbohrer Setra S210H	Kassbohrer Optimal	C35F	1992	Taylor, Frimley, 1996
L7BKM	Scania K113CRB	Van Hool Alizee HE	C49FT	1994	
L10DJT	Scania K113CRB	Van Hool Alizee HE	C53F	1994	D & J, Silvertown, 1997

Previous Registrations:- **GVS385** B238ANK   **TVS986** D238MKX

Livery:- White with three tone blue relief or light brown with grey, red and orange relief.

BRENTS

Metroline Travel Ltd, 118-122 College Road, Harrow, Middlesex, HA1 1DB

					Previous Owner
YLU910X	Leyland Leopard PSU5C/4R	Duple Dominant III	C57F	1982	Smith, Stanmore, 1994
D353RCY	DAF SB2300DHTD585	Plaxton Paramount 3200 II	C53F	1986	Nelson, Glyn-Neath,1995
D542GFH	DAF SB2300DHS585	Plaxton Paramount 3200 III	C53F	1987	Bennett, Gloucester, 1994
G971KJX	DAF MB230LB615	Van Hool Alizee H	C51FT	1990	Robinson, Great Harwood, 1994
K318FYG	Mercedes-Benz 811D	Optare StarRider	C29F	1993	
K712GBE	Mercedes-Benz 410D	Autobus Classique	M12	1993	
K720GBE	Mercedes-Benz 811D	Autobus Classique	C23F	1993	
7804PP	Mercedes-Benz 811D	Autobus Classique	C23F	1994	
L671PWT	Mercedes-Benz 811D	Optare StarRider	C29F	1994	
M840MEE	Mercedes-Benz 410D	Autobus Classique	C12F	1995	
M633UCT	Mercedes-Benz 811D	Autobus Classique	C23F	1995	
M644UCT	Mercedes-Benz 811D	Autobus Classique	C23F	1995	
M626RCP	DAF MB230LT615	Van Hool Alizee HE	C51FT	1995	
N464BHE	Dennis Javelin 12SDA2155	Plaxton Premiere 320	C53F	1995	
N10JET	Dennis Javelin 12SDA2155	Plaxton Premiere 320	C53F	1995	
N20JET	Dennis Javelin 12SDA2155	Plaxton Premiere 320	C53F	1995	
N989AEF	Mercedes-Benz 814D	Autobus Classique	C29F	1996	
N330BAJ	Mercedes-Benz 814D	Autobus Classique	C29F	1996	
N963DWJ	Volvo B10M-62	Plaxton Premiere 350	C51FT	1996	
N964DWJ	Volvo B10M-62	Plaxton Premiere 350	C51FT	1996	
N965DWJ	Volvo B10M-62	Plaxton Premiere 350	C51FT	1996	
N966DWJ	Volvo B10M-62	Plaxton Premiere 350	C51FT	1996	

N254WDO	Mercedes-Benz 814D	Autobus Classique Nouvelle	C29F	1996	
N979WJL	Mercedes-Benz 814D	Autobus Classique Nouvelle	C29F	1996	
N980WJL	Mercedes-Benz 711D	Autobus Classique Nouvelle	C23F	1996	
P845WUG	Volvo B10M-62	Van Hool Alizee HE	C48FT	1997	
P846WUG	Volvo B10M-62	Van Hool Alizee HE	C48FT	1997	

The Metroline Travel bus fleet can be found in the *London Bus Handbook*.

Previous Registrations:-

7804PP	L959JFU				
YLU910X	OKY823X, CBA1L	**D353RCY**	D882BDF, PJI3547	**D542GFH**	D287XCX, PSV111

Livery:- White

BRENTON'S OF BLACKHEATH

C. Clark, 55-57 Invicta Road, Blackheath, London, SE3 7HD   *Previous Owner*

SJI9332	Leyland Leopard PCU3C/4R	Duple Dominant	C51F	1975	Kenzie, Shepreth, 1980
SVA924S	Bedford YMT	Plaxton Supreme III	C49DL	1978	Classical, Beeston, 1988
IDZ2733	Leyland Leopard PSU3E/4R	Plaxton Supreme III	C53F	1978	Cosgrove, Invergowrie, 1981
IDZ2734	Leyland Leopard PSU3E/4R	Plaxton Supreme III	C53F	1978	Cosgrove, Invergowrie, 1981
IDZ2732	Leyland Leopard PSU3E/4R	Duple Dominant II	C53F	1978	Wallace Arnold, 1984
IDZ2736	Leyland Leopard PSU3E/4R	Plaxton Supreme III	C53F	1978	Hamilton, Uxbridge, 1984
IDZ2737	Leyland Leopard PSU3F/4R	Plaxton Supreme IV	C53F	1980	Wallace Arnold, 1986
SJI9328	Mercedes-Benz L608D	Pilcher-Greene	C16FL	1984	Fleet Systems, Woolwich, 1987
SJI9330	Mercedes-Benz L608D	Reeve Burgess	C19F	1984	Mondial, Lewisham, 1989
SJI9331	Mercedes-Benz L608D	Plaxton Mini-Supreme	C25F	1985	
SJI9329	Mercedes-Benz L608D	Plaxton Mini-Supreme	C20F	1986	Epsom Coaches, 1990
D122HML	Mercedes-Benz L608D	Reeve Burgess	C19F	1986	Debonair, Battersea, 1997
901CDU	Volvo B10M-46	Plaxton Paramount 3200 II	C39F	1987	Bere Regis, Dorchester, 1994
KBZ7144	Dennis Javelin 12SDA1907	Duple 320	C53FL	1988	M Track, Crayford, 1996

Previous Registrations:-

IDZ2732	XWX185S	**IDZ2736**	YPP319S	**SJI9328**	A600TGO	**SJI9331**	B276AMG
IDZ2733	TTS883S	**IDZ2737**	LUA291V	**SJI9329**	C201KGJ	**SJI9332**	HVA111N
IDZ2734	TTS884S	**KBZ7144**	E449AGH	**SJI9330**	B521WYU		

Livery:- Cream with red and grey relief.

Special livery:- SVA924S is light blue with two tone brown relief.

CABIN

P.J. Martin, 1 Parsonage Close, Hayes, Middlesex, UB3 2LZ   *Previous Owner*

Reg	Chassis	Body	Seating	Year	Previous Owner
E757HJF	Dennis Javelin 12SDA1907	Duple 320	C57F	1988	Unique, Brighton, 1994
E758HJF	Dennis Javelin 12SDA1907	Duple 320	C53F	1988	Alpha, Brighton, 1993
E635NEL	Dennis Javelin 12SDA1906	Duple 320	C53F	1988	Vince, Burghclere, 1994
P533LNF	LDV Convoy	Concept	M16	1997	

Livery:- White with blue and grey relief.

CANTABRICA

Cantabrica Coaches Ltd, 146-148 London Road, St. Albans, Hertfordshire, AL1 1PQ   *Previous Owner*

Reg	Chassis	Body	Seating	Year	Previous Owner
NPD108L	Leyland National 1151/2R		N/A	1972	Alder Valley South, 1992

	Volvo B10M-60	Berkhof Excellence 2000 HL	C50FT	1992	

J100CCH	J200CCH	J300CCH	J400CCH	J500CCH	K600CCH

Reg	Chassis	Body	Seating	Year
K700CCH	Volvo B10M-60	Berkhof Excellence 2000 HL	C50FT	1993
K800CCH	Volvo B10M-60	Berkhof Excellence 2000 HL	C50FT	1993
K900CCH	Volvo B10M-60	Berkhof Excellence 2000 HL	C50FT	1993
K999CCH	Volvo B10M-60	Berkhof Excellence 2000 HL	C48FT	1993
L7CCH	Volvo B10M-62	Berkhof Excellence 2000 HL	C50FT	1994
L8CCH	Volvo B10M-62	Berkhof Excellence 2000 HL	C50FT	1994
L9CCH	Volvo B10M-62	Berkhof Excellence 2000 HL	C50FT	1994
L10CCH	Volvo B10M-62	Berkhof Excellence 2000 HL	C46FT	1994
M7CCH	Volvo B10M-62	Berkhof Excellence 2000 HL	C50FT	1995
M8CCH	Volvo B10M-62	Berkhof Excellence 2000 HL	C50FT	1995
M9CCH	Volvo B10M-62	Berkhof Excellence 2000 HL	C50FT	1995
M10CCH	Volvo B10M-62	Berkhof Excellence 2000 HL	C50FT	1995
N20CCH	Peugeot Boxer	Cymric	M16	1996

Note:- NPD108L is non-PSV and is used as a hospitality vehicle

Previous Registration:- **K600CCH**   K771XRO

Livery:-   Navy blue and red.

CAPITAL

Capital Logistics Ltd, Sipson Road, West Drayton, Middlesex, UB7 0HN

Reg	Chassis	Body		Seating	Year	*Previous Owner*
XRB417L	Leyland National 1151/2R/0403			B27D	1973	Gatwick Handling, 1992
LLU577P	Leyland National 11351/3R			B33DO	1975	Whyte, West Drayton, 1996
LLU583P	Leyland National 11351/3R			B33DO	1975	Whyte, West Drayton, 1996
OJD877R	Leyland National 10351A/2R			B24D	1977	Heron, Crawley, 1995
TBY111R	Leyland National 11351A/3R			B33DO	1977	Whyte, West Drayton, 1996
TBY112R	Leyland National 11351A/3R			B33DO	1977	Whyte, West Drayton, 1996
TBY125R	Leyland National 11351A/3R			B33DO	1977	Whyte, West Drayton, 1996
THX214S	Leyland National 10351A/2R			B24D	1978	Glynglen, Finchley, 1992
THX229S	Leyland National 10351A/2R			B24D	1978	Glynglen, Finchley, 1992
WGY583S	Leyland National 11351A/3R			B33DO	1978	Whyte, West Drayton, 1996
WGY584S	Leyland National 11351A/3R			B33DO	1978	Whyte, West Drayton, 1996
WGY590S	Leyland National 11351A/3R			B33DO	1978	Whyte, West Drayton, 1996
EGT459T	Leyland National 11351A/3R			B33DO	1978	Whyte, West Drayton, 1996
AYR320T	Leyland National 10351A/2R			B21DL	1979	Kentish Bus, 1995
5304MC	Volvo B10M-61	Plaxton Paramount 3500		C28FT	1984	Marton, West Drayton, 1987
C206TLF	Volvo B10M-61(shortened)	Plaxton Paramount 3200 II		C43F	1985	
C257TLF	Volvo B10M-46	Plaxton Paramount 3200 II		C35F	1985	

	Scania N112DRB	Van Hool Alizee L		DP30D	1987	
E223FLD	E225FLD	E227FLD	E229FLD	E231FLD	E233FLD	
E224FLD	E226FLD	E228FLD	E230FLD	E232FLD		

Reg	Chassis	Body	Seating	Year	*Previous Owner*
E834EUT	Mercedes-Benz 307D	Yeates	M8	1987	AMR, Bedfont, 1995
E625FLD	Mercedes-Benz 609D	Reeve Burgess	B16F	1988	
E322PMD	Volvo B10M-46	Plaxton Derwent II	B31C	1988	Ralph's, Langley, 1993
E323PMD	Volvo B10M-46	Plaxton Derwent II	B31C	1988	Speedlink, 1995
E324PMD	Volvo B10M-46	Plaxton Derwent II	B31C	1988	Ralph's, Langley, 1993
E325PMD	Volvo B10M-46	Plaxton Derwent II	B31C	1988	Ralph's, Langley, 1993
F28NLE	Volvo B10M-46	Plaxton Paramount 3200 III	C39F	1988	Marton, West Drayton, 1993
F29NLE	Volvo B10M-46	Plaxton Paramount 3200 III	C39F	1988	Marton, West Drayton, 1993
F30NLE	Volvo B10M-46	Plaxton Paramount 3200 III	C39F	1988	Marton, West Drayton, 1993
F157NLE	Volvo B10M-46	Plaxton Paramount 3200 III	C35F	1988	Marton, West Drayton, 1993
F292OTL	Freight-Rover Sherpa	Freight-Rover	M16	1989	AMR, Bedfont, 1995
7572MW	Kassbohrer Setra S210HD	Kassbohrer Tornado	C35F	1989	
8325MW	Kassbohrer Setra S215HD	Kassbohrer Tornado	C49FT	1989	
9466MW	Kassbohrer Setra S210HD	Kassbohrer Tornado	C35F	1989	

Reg	Chassis		Body	Seating	Year	History
	DAF SB220LC590		Hispano	B45D	1990	Trans Island Bus Services, Singapore, 1997
G126CLE	G247CLE	G293CLE	G365CLE	G387CLE		
G79BLD	Volvo B10M-60		Plaxton Paramount 3200 III	C53F	1990	KF Cars, Gatwick, 1991
G81BLD	Volvo B10M-60		Plaxton Paramount 3200 III	C53F	1990	KF Cars, Gatwick, 1991
G82BLD	Volvo B10M-60		Plaxton Paramount 3200 III	C53F	1990	KF Cars, Gatwick, 1991
G83BLD	Volvo B10M-60		Plaxton Paramount 3200 III	C53F	1990	KF Cars, Gatwick, 1991
G144BLD	Volvo B10M-46		Plaxton Paramount 3200 III	C43F	1990	Marton, West Drayton, 1993
G145BLD	Volvo B10M-46		Plaxton Paramount 3200 III	C43F	1990	Marton, West Drayton, 1993
1816MW	Kassbohrer Setra S215HD		Kassbohrer Tornado	C49FT	1990	
3262MW	Kassbohrer Setra S215HD		Kassbohrer Tornado	C49FT	1990	
G720XLO	Kassbohrer Setra S215HR		Kassbohrer Rational	C53F	1990	
G801XLO	Volvo B10M-60		Plaxton Paramount 3200 III	C53F	1990	
G802XLO	Volvo B10M-60		Plaxton Paramount 3200 III	C53F	1990	
G803XLO	Volvo B10M-46		Plaxton Paramount 3200 III	C43F	1990	Marton, West Drayton, 1993
G804XLO	Volvo B10M-46		Plaxton Paramount 3200 III	C43F	1990	Marton, West Drayton, 1993
H391SYG	Mercedes-Benz 811D		Optare StarRider	C29F	1990	Marksman, Crawley, 1995
H843UUA	DAF SB220LC550		Optare Delta	B32D	1990	Speedlink, 1995
1093MW	Kassbohrer Setra S215HR		Kassbohrer Rational	C53F	1991	
5579MW	Kassbohrer Setra S215HR		Kassbohrer Rational	C35DL	1991	
9679MW	Kassbohrer Setra S215HR		Kassbohrer Rational	C53F	1991	
	Volvo B10M-60		Plaxton Paramount 3200 III	C53F	1991	Shearings, 1995
H931DRJ	H934DRJ	H936DRJ	H938DRJ	H939DRJ	H940DRJ	
H932DRJ	H935DRJ					
H684FLD	Kassbohrer Setra S215HRI		Kassbohrer Rational	C49FT	1991	
H716FLD	Volvo B10M-46		Plaxton Paramount 3200 III	C43F	1991	Marton, West Drayton, 1993
H717FLD	Volvo B10M-46		Plaxton Paramount 3200 III	C43F	1991	Marton, West Drayton, 1993
H837GLD	Mercedes-Benz 609D		North West Coach Sales	B13F	1991	Marton, West Drayton, 1992
	DAF SB220LC550		Optare Delta	DP37DO	1991	Whyte, West Drayton, 1997
H392SYG	H393SYG	H394SYG	H395SYG	H396SYG		
A5COP	Mercedes-Benz 811D		Optare StarRider	C25F	1992	
J329LLK	Volvo B10M-46		Plaxton Paramount 3200 III	C43F	1992	Marton, West Drayton, 1993
J330LLK	Volvo B10M-46		Plaxton Paramount 3200 III	C43F	1992	Marton, West Drayton, 1993
J331LLK	Volvo B10M-46		Plaxton Paramount 3200 III	C43F	1992	Marton, West Drayton, 1993
J332LLK	Volvo B10M-46		Plaxton Paramount 3200 III	C43F	1992	Marton, West Drayton, 1993
J432LLK	Volvo B10M-60		Plaxton Paramount 3200 III	C53F	1992	
J433LLK	Volvo B10M-60		Plaxton Paramount 3200 III	C53F	1992	

Reg	Chassis	Body	Seating	Year	Notes
K40CAP	Volvo B10M-46	Plaxton Premiere 320	C43F	1993	
K50CAP	Volvo B10M-46	Plaxton Premiere 320	C43F	1993	
K60CAP	Volvo B10M-46	Plaxton Premiere 320	C43F	1993	
K70CAP	Volvo B10M-46	Plaxton Premiere 320	C43F	1993	
K80CAP	Volvo B10M-46	Plaxton Premiere 320	C43F	1993	
K90CAP	Volvo B10M-60	Plaxton Premiere 320	C53F	1993	
K100CAP	Volvo B10M-60	Plaxton Premiere 320	C53F	1993	
K200CAP	Volvo B10M-60	Plaxton Premiere 320	C53F	1993	
K400CAP	Volvo B10M-60	Plaxton Premiere 320	C53F	1993	
K500CAP	Volvo B10M-60	Plaxton Premiere 320	C53F	1993	
K2NCP	Mercedes-Benz 811D	Plaxton Beaver	B23F	1993	
K3NCP	Mercedes-Benz 811D	Plaxton Beaver	B23F	1993	
K4NCP	Mercedes-Benz 811D	Plaxton Beaver	B23F	1993	
K5NCP	Mercedes-Benz 811D	Plaxton Beaver	B23F	1993	
L6NCP	Dennis Dart 9SDL3011	Plaxton Pointer	B25D	1993	
L7NCP	Dennis Dart 9SDL3011	Plaxton Pointer	B25D	1993	
L8NCP	Dennis Dart 9SDL3011	Plaxton Pointer	B25D	1993	
L9NCP	Dennis Dart 9SDL3011	Plaxton Pointer	B25D	1993	
L204ULX	Mercedes-Benz 709D	Plaxton Beaver	B18FL	1993	
L205ULX	Mercedes-Benz 709D	Plaxton Beaver	B18FL	1993	
L206ULX	Mercedes-Benz 709D	Plaxton Beaver	B18FL	1993	
L267ULX	Dennis Dart 9SDL3011	Plaxton Pointer	B25D	1993	
L268ULX	Dennis Dart 9SDL3011	Plaxton Pointer	B25D	1993	
L269ULX	Dennis Dart 9SDL3011	Plaxton Pointer	B25D	1993	
L270ULX	Dennis Dart 9SDL3011	Plaxton Pointer	B25D	1993	
L30CAP	Volvo B10M-62	Jonckheere Deauville 45L	C28FT	1994	
L701CNR	Toyota Coaster HZB50R	Caetano Optimo III	C18F	1994	
L702CNR	Toyota Coaster HZB50R	Caetano Optimo III	C18F	1994	
L703CNR	Toyota Coaster HZB50R	Caetano Optimo III	C18F	1994	
L704CNR	Toyota Coaster HZB50R	Caetano Optimo III	C18F	1994	
M960SDP	Dennis Lance SLF 11SDA3205	Berkhof 2000	B33D	1995	Speedlink, 1997
M962SDP	Dennis Lance SLF 11SDA3205	Berkhof 2000	B33D	1995	Speedlink, 1997

	Mercedes-Benz 208D	Concept	M8	1995	
M536XFY	M537XFY	M541XFY	M542XFY	M543XFY	M544XFY

	Toyota Coaster HZB50R	Caetano Optimo III	C18F	1995	
N791ORY	N792ORY	N793ORY	N794ORY	N795ORY	

	Kassbohrer Setra S250	Kassbohrer Special	C45F	1995	
4019MW					
4967MW	Kassbohrer Setra S250	Kassbohrer Special	C48FT	1995	

5141MW	Kassbohrer Setra S250		Kassbohrer Special	C48FT	1995	
6764MW	Kassbohrer Setra S250		Kassbohrer Special	C44FT	1995	
7639MW	Kassbohrer Setra S250		Kassbohrer Special	C44FT	1995	
N647DFY	Mercedes-Benz Sprinter 208D		Concept	M8	1996	
N648DFY	Mercedes-Benz Sprinter 208D		Concept	M8	1996	
658COP	Dennis Dart SLF SFD212BR1TGW1		Wright Crusader	DP29F	1996	

	Kassbohrer Setra S250		Kassbohrer Special	C53F	1996	
1068MW	1335MW	3401MW	5877MW	5948MW	6963MW	

P2CAP	Volvo B10M-62	Plaxton Premiere 320	C53F	1996	
P3CAP	Volvo B10M-62	Plaxton Premiere 320	C53F	1996	
P4CAP	Volvo B10M-62	Plaxton Premiere 320	C49FT	1996	
P6CAP	Volvo B10M-62	Plaxton Premiere 320	C49FT	1996	
P255MLE	Mercedes-Benz 709D	Plaxton Beaver	B20FL	1997	
P111CAP	Dennis Dart SLF SFD212BR1TGW1	Wright Crusader	DP29F	1997	
P423MLE	Dennis Dart SLF SFD212BR1TGW1	Plaxton Pointer	B31F	1997	
P479MLE	Dennis Dart SLF SFD212BR1TGW1	Plaxton Pointer	B31F	1997	
P480MLE	Dennis Dart SLF SFD212BR1TGW1	Plaxton Pointer	B31F	1997	
P456MLE	Mercedes-Benz 709D	Plaxton Beaver	B20FL	1997	
P566MLE	Volvo B10M-62	Plaxton Premiere 320	C53F	1997	
R956RCH	Volvo B10M-48	Plaxton Premiere 320	C41F	1997	
R957RCH	Volvo B10M-48	Plaxton Premiere 320	C41F	1997	
R958RCH	Volvo B10M-48	Plaxton Premiere 320	C41F	1997	
R959RCH	Volvo B10M-48	Plaxton Premiere 320	C41F	1997	

Previous Registrations:-

EGT459T	WGO597S	**B435RLO**	1335MW	**3262MW**	G719XLO	**E346MLC**	1068MW	**L269ULX**	L5NCP
B433RLO	6963MW	**5304MC**	A999GLD	**7572MW**	9466MW	**L267ULX**	L3NCP	**L270ULX**	L4NCP
B434RLO	5948MW	**1816MW**	G718XLO	**9466MW**	7572MW	**L268ULX**	L2NCP		

Livery:- Blue and white with red relief.

Special Liveries:-

British Airports Authority (White with two tone grey and green relief) :- A545WGP, C302FML, M960SDP, M962SDP, P423MLE, P479MLE, P480MLE
Copthorne Hotel (white):- A5COP
Flightpath (White with blue and grey):- E223-233FLD, E322-5PMD.
Forte Post Hotel (Dark Blue):- P111CAP
Hounslow Hoppa (White and green) :- H837GLD, L204-206ULX, P255MLE, P456MLE
National Car Parks (Yellow and white):- E625FLD, K2-5NCP
NCP Gatwick (Blue and white):-L267-70ULX, L6-9NCP
Silver blue with red and blue:- L30CAP
White and dark green:- H392-6SYG

CAVALIER TOURS

P. Phillips, 10 Waterside Close, Barking, Essex, IG11 9EQ

					Previous Owner
HDZ1764	Scania K112CRS	Jonckheere Jubilee P599	C51FT	1983	Brooks, Kendal, 1996
VIB7660	Bova EL26/581	Bova Europa	C53F	1983	APT, Rayleigh, 1996
MIL9583	Mercedes-Benz 0303/15R	Mercedes-Benz	C49FT	1985	Guideline, Wimbledon, 1997

Livery:- Dark blue with white relief.

Previous Registrations:-

HDZ1764 DLX34Y   **MIL9583** 929ECH   **VIB7660** OOU854Y, LIB4333, PMS371, PMS1M, APT416B

CAVALIER

A.W. Pagan, 87 Fleetside, West Molesey, Surrey, KT8 2NG

N782ORY	Toyota Coaster HZB50R	Caetano Optimo III	C18F	1996
N783ORY	Toyota Coaster HZB50R	Caetano Optimo III	C18F	1996
N588TAY	Iveco ECO3.CC.95	Indcar 80	C34F	1996
P431JDT	Dennis Javelin 10SDA2139	Plaxton Premiere 320	C43F	1996
R507SCH	Iveco Eurorider 391-12-35	Beulas Stergo E	C49FT	1997

Livery:- White with blue signwriting (R507SCH is white and blue).

CENTURION

R. Barnett, 39 Rycroft, Windsor, Berkshire, SL4 4HQ

					Previous Owner
E238HCD	Volvo B10M-61	Jonckheere Jubilee P599	C51FT	1988	Rambler, Hastings, 1997
N249NNR	MAN 18-370	Caetano Algarve II	C53F	1996	

Previous Registration:- **E238HCD**   E697NNH, HSK834, TDY388

Liveries:- Green and black with cream relief (E238HCD) or white (N249NNR).

CHALFONT

Chalfont Coaches of Harrow Ltd, 200 Featherstone Road, Southall, Middlesex, UB2 5AQ

					Previous Owner
WBB330T	Volvo B58-61	Plaxton Supreme IV	C57F	1979	Wansbeck, Ashington, 1985
MNT595W	Volvo B58-56	Plaxton Supreme IV Express	C53F	1981	Vagg, Knockin Heath, 1983
SGS510W	Volvo B58-61	Plaxton Viewmaster IV	C36FT	1981	Burrows, Hounslow, 1986

E329FLD	Volvo B10M-61	Plaxton Paramount 3200 III	C57F	1987	
F306RMH	Volvo B10M-61	Plaxton Paramount 3500 III	C57F	1987	
F896NWC	Freight-Rover Sherpa	Adams	C16F	1988	Fisher, Deadmans Cross, 1993
H158DJU	Volvo B10M-60	Plaxton Paramount 3200 III	C57F	1990	
H426DVM	Peugeot-Talbot Express	Made to Measure	M12	1990	Fisher, Deadmans Cross, 1993
L253LDT	Leyland-DAF 400	Autobus Classique	C16F	1993	
M886SKU	LDV 400	Autobus Classique	C16F	1994	
M860TYC	Volvo B10M-62	Van Hool Alizee HE	C46FT	1994	
M861TYC	Volvo B10M-62	Van Hool Alizee HE	C53FT	1994	
M862TYC	Volvo B10M-62	Van Hool Alizee HE	C57F	1994	
N197DYB	Volvo B10M-62	Van Hool Alizee HE	C57F	1996	
N198DYB	Volvo B10M-62	Van Hool Alizee HE	C49FT	1996	
P938EHN	Mercedes-Benz 814D	Autobus Classique	C29F	1997	

Livery:- White and purple.

CHALFONT LINE

The Chalfont Line Ltd, 4 Medway Parade, Perivale, Middlesex, UB6 8HR   *Previous Owner*

LIB5949	Volvo B10M-61	Plaxton Paramount 3200 II	C45DL	1986	O'Conner, Hanwell, 1990
E608AWA	Mercedes-Benz L608D	Whittaker	C23FL	1988	Gosling, Redbourn, 1993
G293DOV	Renault Master	Jubilee (1993)	M10L	1990	private owner, 1993
G962UKE	Renault Master	Jubilee (1994)	M16L	1990	private owner, 1994
H512BND	Mercedes-Benz 609D	Made To Measure	C23FL	1990	Oates, Smallfield, 1991
K228TRG	DAF 400	Jubilee	M10L	1993	
K229TRG	DAF 400	Jubilee	M11L	1993	
K764WUE	DAF 400	Jubilee	M16	1993	
L531YHA	DAF 400	Jubilee	M16L	1993	
L532YHA	DAF 400	Jubilee	M16L	1993	
L533YHA	DAF 400	Jubilee	M8L	1993	
L941CJW	Renault Master	Jubilee	M9L	1993	
L942CJW	Renault Master	Jubilee	M8L	1993	
L883CJW	Renault Master	Jubilee	M7L	1994	
M354HOX	Renault Master	Jubilee	M7L	1994	
N578SOA	Renault Master	Jubilee	M3L	1995	
P930KYC	Volvo B10M-62	Van Hool Alizee HE	C44DTL	1997	

Note:- P930KYC is convertible to 36 seats with 3 wheelchairs or 24 seats with 8 wheelchairs.

Previous Registration:- **LIB5949**   C211FMF

Named vehicles:- LIB5949   Liberator VI   P930KYC   Millennium Executive

Livery:- White.   Special livery:- P930KYC is black.

CHANNEL COACHWAYS/SUPREME CAR HIRE

Cherrybriar Ltd, Supreme House, Stour Wharf, Stour Road, Bow, London, E3 2NT

Reg	Chassis	Body	Seating	Year	Previous Owner
J503LRY	Toyota Coaster HDB30R	Caetano Optimo II	C18F	1991	Capital, West Drayton, 1997
M534TVH	LDV 400	Concept	M16	1995	
N11CHN	Scania K113TRB	Irizar Century 12.37	C51FT	1996	
N12CHN	Iveco Eurorider 391-12-29	Beulas Stergo E	C49FT	1996	
N180OUT	Iveco ECO3.CC.95	Indcar 80	C33F	1996	Cavalier, West Molesey, 1996
P383ARY	Iveco Eurorider 391-12-35	Beulas Stergo E	C49FT	1996	
P270SHK	Toyota Coaster BB50R	Caetano Optimo IV	C21F	1997	

Livery:- Metallic maroon.

CHIVERS COACHES

Chivers Coaches Ltd, 13a Ross Parade, Wallington, Surrey, SM6 8QG

Reg	Chassis	Body	Seating	Year	Previous Owner
ESU264	Bedford YMP	Plaxton Paramount 3200	C38F	1984	Armchair, Brentford, 1990
PAZ7314	DAF SB2300DHTD585	Plaxton Paramount 3200	C53F	1985	Nightingale, Langley, 1995
PAZ7315	DAF SB2300DHTD585	Plaxton Paramount 3200 III	C53F	1987	Herrington, Alderholt, 1997
F208PTL	Freight-Rover Sherpa	Chassis Developments	C16F	1989	Guymers, Lincoln, 1997
G836VAY	Toyota Coaster HB31R	Caetano Optimo	C21F	1989	Ross, Wrexham 1992

Previous Registrations:- **ESU264** A842PPP   **PAZ7314** B545MLN   **PAZ7315** D631YCX, 2159CD, D713LEL

Livery:- Silver, blue and white.

CLAREMONT

Claremont Coaches Ltd, 246 Longfellow Road, Worcester Park, Surrey, KT4 8AT

Reg	Chassis	Body	Seating	Year	Previous Owner
GPA616V	Volvo B58-56	Plaxton Supreme IV	C53F	1980	Sheenway, Sheen, 1984
YGT619W	Volvo B58-56	Plaxton Supreme IV	C53F	1981	Sheenway, Sheen, 1985
UXI7897	Volvo B10M-61	Duple Dominant IV	C53F	1983	Buffalo, Flitwick, 1996
LBZ2301	Volvo B10M-61	Plaxton Paramount 3200 II	C53F	1985	Alpha, Brighton, 1997
RBZ2673	Volvo B10M-61	Plaxton Paramount 3200 III	C53F	1987	Excelsior, Bournemouth, 1989
RBZ2674	Volvo B10M-61	Plaxton Paramount 3200 III	C53F	1987	Excelsior, Bournemouth, 1989
RBZ2675	Volvo B10M-61	Plaxton Paramount 3200 III	C53F	1987	Excelsior, Bournemouth, 1989
F489WPR	Toyota Coaster HB31R	Caetano Optimo	C18F	1989	

Previous Registrations:- **LBZ2301** B914SPR   **RBZ2674** D266HFX, XEL158, D571KJT   **UXI7897** ENF582Y
RBZ2673 D268HFX, XEL31, D570KJT   **RBZ2675** D265HFX, XEL941, D572KJT

Livery:- White and turquoise with ochre relief.

CLARKES OF LONDON

E. Clarke & Son (Coaches) Ltd, Kangley Bridge Road, Lower Sydenham, London, SE26 5AT

					Previous Owner
BIL1124	Volvo B10M-53	Plaxton Paramount 4000RS II	CH54/13CT	1986	Flights, Birmingham, 1990
BIL1816	Volvo B10M-53	Plaxton Paramount 4000RS II	CH54/13CT	1986	Flights, Birmingham, 1990
D106BNV	Volvo B10M-61	Jonckheere Jubilee P50	C53F	1987	
D107BNV	Volvo B10M-61	Jonckheere Jubilee P50	C53F	1987	
D24CNR	Volvo B10M-61	Van Hool Alizee H	C53F	1987	
D25CNR	Volvo B10M-61	Van Hool Alizee H	C53F	1987	
BIL1977	Volvo B10M-61	Van Hool Alizee H	C49FT	1987	Excelsior, Bournemouth, 1992
E217JJF	Volvo B10M-61	Van Hool Alizee H	C53F	1988	
BIL1878	Volvo B10M-61	Van Hool Alizee H	C49FT	1988	Excelsior, Bournemouth, 1992
F167RJF	Volvo B10M-60	Van Hool Alizee H	C53F	1989	
F171RJF	Volvo B10M-60	Van Hool Alizee H	C53F	1989	
F672TFH	Volvo B10M-60	Van Hool Alizee H	C53F	1989	
F673TFH	Volvo B10M-60	Van Hool Alizee H	C53F	1989	
J451HDS	Volvo B10M-60	Van Hool Alizee H	C49FT	1992	Park, Hamilton, 1992
J454HDS	Volvo B10M-60	Van Hool Alizee H	C49FT	1992	Park, Hamilton, 1992

	Volvo B10M-62	Van Hool Alizee HE	C49FT	1994

L100CLA	L200CLA	L300CLA	L400CLA	L500CLA

L600CLA	Volvo B10M-62	Jonckheere Deauville 45	C53F	1994
L700CLA	Volvo B10M-62	Jonckheere Deauville 45	C53F	1994
L800CLA	Volvo B10M-62	Jonckheere Deauville 45	C53F	1994
L900CLA	Volvo B10M-62	Jonckheere Deauville 45	C53F	1994
M111CLA	Volvo B12T	Jonckheere Monaco	CH57/14CT	1995
M222CLA	Volvo B12T	Jonckheere Monaco	CH57/14CT	1995

	Volvo B10M-62	Jonckheere Deauville 45	C53F	1995

M321KRY	M323KRY	M325KRY	M327KRY	M328KRY	M329KRY	M333CLA
M322KRY	M324KRY	M326KRY				

N444CLA	Volvo B10M-62	Jonckheere Mistral 50	C49FT	1995
N555CLA	Volvo B10M-62	Jonckheere Deauville 45	C53F	1996

	Volvo B10M-62	Jonckheere Deauville 45	C49FT	1996

N532SJF	N533SJF	N534SJF	N535SJF	N536SJF	N537SJF	N538SJF

	Volvo B10M-62		Jonckheere Deauville 45	C53F	1996		
N539SJF	N542SJF	N545SJF	N547SJF	N549SJF	N551SJF	N553SJF	
N540SJF	N543SJF	N546SJF	N548SJF	N550SJF	N552SJF	N554SJF	
N541SJF	N544SJF						

P77COL	Volvo B12T	Jonckheere Monaco	CH57/14CT	1997
P88COL	Volvo B12T	Jonckheere Monaco	CH57/14CT	1997
P99COL	Volvo B10M-62	Jonckheere Mistral 50	C53F	1997

	Volvo B10M-62		Jonckheere Mistral 50	C53F	1997
P241AUT	P242AUT	P243AUT	P244AUT	P245AUT	

Coaches currently on hire from Yeates (dealer):-

M627FNS	Volvo B10M-60	Jonckheere Deauville 45	C49FT	1995
M628FNS	Volvo B10M-60	Jonckheere Deauville 45	C49FT	1995
M629FNS	Volvo B10M-60	Jonckheere Deauville 45	C49FT	1995
M630FNS	Volvo B10M-60	Jonckheere Deauville 45	C49FT	1995
N808NHS	Volvo B10M-62	Jonckheere Deauville 45	C49FT	1996

Currently on loan from Kassbohrer of Lincoln:-

P49YTL	Kassbohrer Setra S250	Kassbohrer Special	C53F	1997

Previous Registrations:-

BIL1124	C720GOP,BIL1214	**BIL1878**	E309OPR	**BIL1977**	GPL-066(Belgium), XEL24, E455SEL
BIL1816	C730GOP				

Livery:- Turquoise and White.

Special liveries:-

M111CLA & M222CLA are white with red relief and carry "Globus" fleetnames.
J451HDS carries "Miki Travel" fleetnames (in Japanese).
All the hired coaches are white.

COLLINS COACHES

Collins Coaches Ltd, Unit 6, Waterside Trading Estate, Trumpers Way, Hanwell, London, W7 2QD

					Previous Owner
JYJ192N	Volvo B58-61	Plaxton Elite III	C57F	1974	Crawley Luxury, 1994
GUR428N	Volvo B58-61	Plaxton Elite III	C53F	1975	Crocker, St. Austell, 1994
HVD728N	Leyland Leopard PSU5/4R	Plaxton Elite III	C57F	1975	Hearn, Harrow, 1996
LHE500P	AEC Reliance 6U3ZR	Plaxton Supreme III	C57F	1976	George, Hare Street ,1983
RLB621R	Volvo B58-61	Plaxton Supreme III	C57F	1976	Hawkins, Ruislip, 1983
TGD997R	Volvo B58-56	Plaxton Supreme III	C53F	1977	GN Coaches, Greenford,1984
XPF856S	Leyland Leopard PSU5/4R	Plaxton Supreme III	C57F	1978	Thomas, West Ewell,1995
MDS232V	Volvo B58-61	Plaxton Supreme IV	C57F	1980	Ford, Gunnislake, 1987
UUR414W	DAF MB200DKTL600	Plaxton Supreme IV	C57F	1981	Shrubb, Tatsfield, 1988
NGT2Y	Volvo B10M-61	Plaxton Paramount 3500	C49F	1983	Epsom Coaches, 1990
A511FRM	Volvo B10M-61	Jonckheere Jubilee P90	CH43/9FT	1984	LA Travel, Laindon, 1992
F795TBC	TAZ D3200	TAZ Dubrava	C49FT	1989	

Previous Registrations:-

A511FRM A283ERM, 890TTE, A511FRM, A511ERM **XPF856S** XKK184S, 8794R
JYJ192N VOR555N, VOI8115

Livery:- Red, grey and white.

CONISTON

R.F. Smock, 88 Coniston Road, Bromley, Kent, BR1 4JB

					Previous Owner
LBZ2952	Leyland Leopard PSU3E/4R	Plaxton Supreme III Express	C53F	1978	Hunter, Seaton Delaval, 1984
BFW251W	Volvo B58-61	Plaxton Supreme IV	C53F	1981	Red Line, Bromley, 1996
LBZ2953	Volvo B10M-56	Plaxton Paramount 3500	C45F	1983	Glenton, Charlton, 1988
G881VNA	Scania K93CRB	Plaxton Paramount 3200 III LS	C53F	1990	Maxfield, Aughton, 1994
G882VNA	Scania K93CRB	Plaxton Paramount 3200 III LS	C53F	1990	Mayne, Clayton, 1994
M952HRY	Dennis Javelin 12SDA2136	Caetano Algarve II	C53F	1994	

Previous Registrations:-

BFW251W JDO667W, KVL261   **LBZ2952** TVK502S   **LBZ2953** PHM180Y

Livery:- White with red fleetnames.

DAVID CORBEL

David Corbel of London Ltd, 6 Camrose Avenue, Edgware, Middlesex, HA8 6EG   *Previous Owner*

BXI477	Van Hool T818	Van Hool Astron	CH49/11FT	1983	Speedbird, Wembley, 1993
BPR99Y	Leyland Tiger TRCTL11/3R	Duple Laser	C57F	1983	Midland Fox, 1996
CBA1L	Leyland Tiger TRCTL11/3R	Duple Laser	C55F	1983	Shaw, Worsborough, 1995
LBZ8368	Auwaerter Neoplan N122/3	Auwaerter Skyliner	CH55/20CT	1984	Elite, Stockport, 1993
UJF396	Auwaerter Neoplan N122/3	Auwaerter Skyliner	CH55/20CT	1984	Elite, Stockport, 1993
620BZ	Auwaerter Neoplan N122/3	Auwaerter Skyliner	CH55/20CT	1984	Ableace, Hoddesdon, 1995
C70AYY	Toyota Coaster BB30R	Caetano Optimo	C20F	1985	Amanda, Bedfont, 1995

Named Vehicles:-

CBA1L	Andy's Super Tiger	LBZ8368	Lady Margaret	UJF396	Little Linda

Previous Registrations:-

BXI477	7256DD, RBD41Y	**UFJ396**	A106MWT
620BZ	A107MWT, VOI9025, HWY701, ACH972A, RRK2	**CBA1L**	UNL448Y
LBZ8368	A102MWT, LSV821, A864RUG, CBA1L		

Livery:- Two tone blue and silver.

CUMFILUX COACHES

N.R. Farrow, 69 Corwell Lane, Hillingdon, Middlesex, UB8 3DE   *Previous Owner*

H15MNM	Scania K113CRB	Berkhof Excellence 2000	C53FT	1991	M & M, Harrow Weald, 1996
L563HNA	Mercedes-Benz 308D	Derwent	C14F	1994	
N88CLC	Mercedes-Benz 814D	Cacciamali Ibis	C25F	1996	

Livery:- White and orange

DP COACHLINES

P.D. Prato, 1 Oakwood Crescent, Greenford, Middlesex, UB6 0RP   *Previous Owner*

WSV508	Van Hool TD824	Van Hool Astramega	CH57/23DT	1983	Thamesroute, Highbury, 1994
G657WEE	Mercedes-Benz 811D	Coachcraft	C21F	1989	G&C, Queens Park, 1992

Previous Registration:- **WSV508** NDS840Y

Livery:- Red, grey and blue.

D & J COACHES OF HARROW

D.J. Horne, 44 St. Thomas Drive, Hatch End, Middlesex, HA5 4SS

P169ANR	Dennis Javelin 12SDA2134	Caetano Algarve II	C53F	1996

Livery:- White.

DAVIAN

Davian Coaches Ltd, 495 Southbury Road, Enfield, Middlesex, EN3 4JW

					Previous Owner
JTM113V	Mercedes-Benz L207D	Reeve Burgess	M12	1979	Franklin, Borehamwood, 1981
XJN202X	Mercedes-Benz L207D	Reeve Burgess	M12	1981	
YJN979X	Mercedes-Benz L207D	Reeve Burgess	M12	1982	
FOO641Y	Mercedes-Benz L207D	Reeve Burgess	M12	1982	
FOO642Y	Mercedes-Benz L207D	Reeve Burgess	M12	1982	
DAZ4299	Leyland Tiger TRCTL11/3R	Plaxton Paramount 3500	C51FT	1983	Daniels, Abridge, 1995
A61SEV	DAF MB200DKFL600	Berkhof Esprite 350	C57F	1984	Ensign, Purfleet, 1984
C634PSW	MAN MT8.136	GC Smith Whippet	C25F	1986	Armstrong, Castle Douglas, 1987
D29CAC	Scania K112CRS	Plaxton Paramount 3200 II LS	C55F	1986	Oakfield, Enfield, 1994
D41MAG	Iveco Daily 49.10	Robin Hood City Nippy	DP16F	1987	County Bus, 1991
E585OEF	Scania K112CRB	Plaxton Paramount 3500 III	C49FT	1988	Aston, Kempsey, 1994
E116XWF	Scania K112CRB	Plaxton Paramount 3500 III	C55F	1988	Brown, South Kirkby, 1996

Previous Registration:- **DAZ4299**   SMU992Y

Livery:- White with orange and blue.

DEBONAIR

Debonair Travel, Battersea Wharf, Chelsea Bridge Road, Battersea, London, SW 8

					Previous Owner
F875RFP	Dennis Javelin 12SDA1907	Duple 320	C53F	1989	Pemico Travel, Peckham, 1997
F84GGC	Mercedes-Benz 811D	Robin Hood	C29F	1989	R & I, North Acton, 1995
G904OWY	Leyland Swift LBM6T/2RSO	Reeve Burgess Harrier	C37F	1990	Poppleton, Pontefract,1994
672DYA	Toyota Coaster HDB30R	Caetano Optimo II	C21F	1991	R & I, North Acton, 1996

Previous Registration:- **672DYA**   J310KFP

Livery:- White with blue relief.

DENNINGS

P.J. Denning, 104 Clydesdale, Enfield, Middlesex, EN3 4RN   *Previous Owner*

CBM458T	Ford Transit	Dormobile	B16FL	1979	private owner, 1993
AVK157V	Leyland Atlantean AN68A/2R	Alexander AL	H49/37F	1980	Busways, 1997
MMC210W	Volvo B58-61	Duple Dominant III	C53F	1981	
PRO431W	Mercedes-Benz L508D	Reeve Burgess	C19F	1981	Angel Motors, Tottenham, 1986
TJI5813	Volvo B58-61	Jonckheere Bermuda	C51F	1981	Penniston, Melton Mowbray, 1984
ULA518X	Ford Transit	Dormobile	B16FL	1982	London Borough of Islington, 1987
PJI2984	Mercedes-Benz L608D	Reeve Burgess	C25F	1982	Toms, Southend, 1996
OMA655Y	Mercedes-Benz L508DG	Devon Conversions	C19F	1983	Dobbins, Barnet, 1988
A312NMJ	Ford Transit	Mellor	B16FL	1983	Chalfont Line, Perivale, 1985
F365MUT	Hestair-Duple 425 SDA1512	Duple 425	C53FT	1988	Steele, Potters Bar, 1991

Previous Registrations:- **MMC210W** FIB4781   **PJI2984** KGG725Y   **TJI5813** VBD569W

Livery:- White with yellow relief.

DIAMOND

Diamond Coaches (Harrow) Ltd, 33 Westbury Avenue, Southall, Middlesex, UB1 2UY   *Previous Owner*

KIJ332	Volvo B10M-61	Jonckheere Jubilee P90	CH48/9DT	1983	Dunn-Line, Nottingham, 1993

Previous Registrations:- **KIJ332** JNV632Y   Livery:- White with black and orange relief.

EBDON'S TOURS

Ebdon's Coaches Ltd, 1-3 Powerscroft Road, Sidcup, Kent, DA14 5DT   *Previous Owner*

1	E993KJF	Mercedes-Benz 0303/15R	Mercedes-Benz	C53F	1988	Redwing, Camberwell, 1996
2	M409TWF	Auwaerter Neoplan N117/3	Auwaerter Spaceliner	CH50/6CT	1994	
3	E995KJF	Mercedes-Benz 0303/15R	Mercedes-Benz	C53F	1988	Redwing, Camberwell, 1996
4	P91VEE	Kassbohrer Setra S250	Kassbohrer Special	C48FT	1997	
5	J41XHE	Auwaerter Neoplan N122/3	Auwaerter Skyliner	CH57/20DT	1991	
6	EFW863X	Auwaerter Neoplan N122/3	Auwaerter Skyliner	CH53/18DT	1982	
7	H178RHE	Auwaerter Neoplan N122/3	Auwaerter Skyliner	CH57/22CT	1990	
8	N685AHL	Scania K113TRB	Irizar Century 12.37	C48FT	1995	
9	L955MWB	Auwaerter Neoplan N116/3	Auwaerter Cityliner	C50FT	1994	
10	MIW4845	Mercedes-Benz 0303/15R	Mercedes-Benz	C49FT	1987	Bergland, Strood, 1997
11	MIW4850	Drogmoller E320	Drogmoller Euro-Pullman	C49FT	1986	Bergland, Strood, 1997
12	MIW4851	Drogmoller E320	Drogmoller Euro-Pullman	C49FT	1986	Bergland, Strood, 1997
14	MIW4844	Mercedes-Benz 0303/15R	Mercedes-Benz	C49FT	1987	Bergland, Strood, 1997
15	MIW4842	Mercedes-Benz 0303/15R	Mercedes-Benz	C49FT	1987	Bergland, Strood, 1997
16	MIW4849	Drogmoller E330	Drogmoller Comet	C49FT	1985	Bergland, Strood, 1997

JGF294K	Daimler Fleetline CRG6	Park Royal	N/A	1972	General Foods, Banbury, 1996
JBO75W	MCW Metrobus DR102/20	MCW	H46/31F	1981	County Bus, 1997
PYH651Y	Leyland Cub CU435	Reeve Burgess	DP32F	1983	Taylor French, Aylesbury, 1997
A963ARD	Mercedes-Benz L608D	Reeve Burgess	C19F	1984	Owen's, Sidcup, 1996
C932SLT	Renault-Dodge G10	Wadham Stringer Vanguard	B39F	1985	British Airways, 1996
C907VLB	Renault-Dodge G10	Wadham Stringer Vanguard	B41F	1986	British Airways, 1996
C908VLB	Renault-Dodge G10	Wadham Stringer Vanguard	DP33F	1986	British Airways, 1996
C909VLB	Renault-Dodge G10	Wadham Stringer Vanguard	B41F	1986	British Airways, 1996
D512CLN	Renault-Dodge G10	Wadham Stringer Vanguard	DP34F	1987	British Airways, 1996
F188RMK	Renault G13	Wadham Stringer Vanguard	B39F	1989	London Borough of Waltham Forest, 1997

Note:- JGF294K is a hospitality unit.

Named vehicles:- Ebdon's Cityliner:- 9   Ebdon's Skyliner:- 5, 6, 7   Ebdon's Spaceliner:- 2

Previous Registrations:-

J41XHE	H156RHE	**MIW4844**	D387BNR	**MIW4849**	B484MLN	**MIW4851**	C868TLF
MIW4842	D641AJF	**MIW4845**	E845EUT	**MIW4850**	C700TLF	**PYH651Y**	PYH651Y,TFO415

Livery:- Claret, white and grey.

P & J ELLIS LTD

P & J. Ellis Ltd, 69 Barn Way, Wembley Park, Middlesex, HA9 9NP

					Previous Owner
G981LRP	Volvo B10M-60	Jonckheere Deauville P599	C51FT	1990	Rowley, Emerson Park, 1993
G143MNH	Volvo B10M-60	Jonckheere Deauville P599	C51FT	1990	Cantabrica, St Albans, 1992
H385HRY	MAN 10.180	Jonckheere Deauville P35	C34FT	1991	Hallmark, Luton, 1996
J9TCC	MAN 10.180	Jonckheere Deauville P35	C30FT	1991	Travellers, Hounslow, 1997
M572DSJ	Volvo B10M-62	Jonckheere Deauville 45	C53F	1995	Park, Hamilton, 1997
M574DSJ	Volvo B10M-62	Jonckheere Deauville 45	C53F	1995	Park, Hamilton, 1997
M945JJU	Volvo B10M-62	Jonckheere Deauville 45L	C51FT	1995	
M946JJU	Volvo B10M-62	Jonckheere Deauville 45L	C51FT	1995	
M947JJU	Volvo B10M-62	Jonckheere Deauville 45L	C57F	1995	

Previous Registrations:-

H385HRY	H404ERP, H4PSW	**M572DSJ**	LSK875	**M574DSJ**	LSK873	**J9TCC**	J2TCC

Livery:- White with red signwriting.

EMPRESS OF LONDON

Empress Motors Ltd, 3 Corbridge Crescent, Bethnal Green, London, E2 9DS

Reg	Chassis	Body	Seating	Year	Previous Owner
323NAA	Bedford YLQ	Duple Dominant II	C45F	1978	Alpha, Brighton, 1980
FSU827	Volvo B10M-61	Plaxton Paramount 3200 II LS	C53F	1986	Excelsior, Bournemouth, 1987
FSU828	Volvo B10M-61	Plaxton Paramount 3200 II LS	C53F	1986	Excelsior, Bournemouth, 1987
PJI1830	Volvo B10M-61	Van Hool Alizee H	C53F	1987	Farrey, Durham, 1994
LJI8024	Volvo B10M-61	Plaxton Paramount 3200 III LS	C57F	1988	
LJI8023	Volvo B10M-61	Plaxton Paramount 3500 III	C53F	1988	
LJI8022	Volvo B10M-60	Plaxton Paramount 3500 III	C57F	1989	
LJI8025	Volvo B10M-60	Plaxton Paramount 3500 III	C53FT	1989	
LJI3521	Volvo B10M-60	Plaxton Paramount 3200 III	C53F	1989	Excelsior, Bournemouth, 1990
PIW2633	Volvo B10M-60	Plaxton Paramount 3500 III	C50F	1990	Wallace Arnold,1994
PJI6431	Volvo B10M-60	Plaxton Paramount 3500 III	C53F	1990	Wallace Arnold,1994
H572CRJ	Ford Transit	Mellor	C16F	1991	Munro, Uddingston, 1993
PIW2632	Volvo B10M-60	Plaxton Paramount 3500 III	C50F	1991	Wallace Arnold, 1994
PIW2634	Volvo B10M-60	Plaxton Paramount 3500 III	C50F	1991	Wallace Arnold, 1994
PIW2635	Toyota Coaster HDR30R	Caetano Optimo II	C21F	1993	Voy, Newton Aycliffe, 1994
M340MRU	Volvo B10M-62	Plaxton Premiere 320	C49FT	1995	Excelsior, Bournemouth, 1996
M394MRU	Volvo B10M-62	Plaxton Premiere 320	C53F	1995	Excelsior, Bournemouth, 1996
M130UWY	Volvo B10M-62	Plaxton Premiere 350	C50F	1995	Wallace Arnold, 1996
SJI8126	MAN 10.180	Jonckheere Deauville P35	C32FT	1991	Andy James, Tetbury, 1991

Previous Registrations:-

323NAA	AAP2T	**LJI8023**	F384MUT	**PIW2633**	G524LWU	**PJI6431**	G552LWU
FSU827	C102AFX	**LJI8024**	E166OMD	**PIW2634**	H623UWR	**SJI8126**	H52XBD
FSU828	C103AFX	**LJI8025**	F718SML	**PIW2635**	K587VBC	**M340MRU**	A12EXC
LJI3521	F472WFX	**PIW2632**	H632UWR	**PJI1830**	D788SGB	**M394MRU**	XEL158
LJI8022	F717SML						

Livery:- Cream with red and black signwriting.

EPSOM COACHES

H.R. Richmond Ltd, Blenheim Road, Longmead, Epsom, Surrey, KT19 9AF

601	F516GGJ	Volvo B10M-60	Van Hool Alizee H	C53F	1989
602	F517GGJ	Volvo B10M-60	Van Hool Alizee H	C53F	1989
603	G518OGP	Volvo B10M-60	Van Hool Alizee H	C53F	1990
604	G519OGP	Volvo B10M-60	Van Hool Alizee H	C53F	1990
605	H531WGH	Volvo B10M-60	Van Hool Alizee H	C53F	1991
606	H532WGH	Volvo B10M-60	Van Hool Alizee H	C53F	1991
607	H533WGH	Volvo B10M-60	Van Hool Alizee H	C53F	1991
608	L231BUT	Dennis Javelin 12SDA2138	Plaxton Premiere 320	C53F	1994
609	L232BUT	Dennis Javelin 12SDA2138	Plaxton Premiere 320	C53F	1994
610	L233BUT	Dennis Javelin 12SDA2138	Plaxton Premiere 320	C53F	1994
611	L234BUT	Dennis Javelin 12SDA2138	Plaxton Premiere 320	C53F	1994
612	M790LPH	Dennis Javelin 12SDA2131	Plaxton Premiere 320	C53F	1995
613	M793LPH	Dennis Javelin 12SDA2131	Plaxton Premiere 320	C53F	1995
701	M332MPG	Dennis Javelin 12SDA2155	Plaxton Premiere 320	C53F	1995
702	N406SPC	Dennis Javelin 12SDA2159	Plaxton Premiere 320	C53F	1996
703	N407SPC	Dennis Javelin 12SDA2159	Plaxton Premiere 320	C53F	1996
704	N408SPC	Dennis Javelin 12SDA2159	Plaxton Premiere 320	C53F	1996
705	N409SPC	Dennis Javelin 12SDA2159	Plaxton Premiere 320	C53F	1996
706	N479VPA	Dennis Javelin SFD721BR3TGJ2	Plaxton Premiere 320	C53F	1996
707	P707DPA	Dennis Javelin SFD731BR3VGJ2	Plaxton Premiere 320	C53F	1997
708	P708DPA	Volvo B10M-62	Jonckheere Mistral 50	C53F	1997
709	P709DPA	Volvo B10M-62	Jonckheere Mistral 50	C53F	1997
710	P710DPA	Volvo B10M-62	Jonckheere Mistral 50	C53F	1997
801	A8HRR	Volvo B10M-60	Van Hool Alizee HE	C49FT	1993
802	A9HRR	Volvo B10M-60	Van Hool Alizee HE	C49FT	1993
803	M791LPH	Dennis Javelin 12SDA2131	Plaxton Premiere 320	C48FT	1995
804	M792LPH	Dennis Javelin 12SDA2131	Plaxton Premiere 320	C48FT	1995
805	N405SPC	Dennis Javelin 12SDA2155	Plaxton Premiere 320	C48FT	1996
806	P806DPA	Volvo B10M-62	Jonckheere Mistral 50	C49FT	1997
807	P807DPA	Volvo B10M-62	Jonckheere Mistral 50	C49FT	1997
901	J721FGP	Toyota Coaster HDB30R	Caetano Optimo II	C18F	1992
902	K460PNR	Toyota Coaster HDB30R	Caetano Optimo II	C18F	1992
903	K465PNR	Toyota Coaster HDB30R	Caetano Optimo II	C18F	1993

Previous Registrations:- **A8HRR** K289GDT, K288GDT **A9HRR** K288GDT, K289GDT.

Livery:- Cream with maroon and black relief.

ESCORT COACHES

Mrs H.M. Friedel, 244 Lincoln Road, Enfield, Middlesex, EN1 1TA

					Previous Owner
137ASV	Leyland Leopard PSU5C/4R	Plaxton Viewmaster IV	C53F	1980	SSS, Euston, 1986
B737PLA	Mercedes-Benz L307D	Devon Conversions	M12	1985	
C598TLM	Mercedes-Benz L307D	Devon Conversions	M12	1985	
A17ESC	MCW Metrorider MF150/73	MCW	C25F	1988	
EX9242	Mercedes-Benz 811D	Optare StarRider	C21F	1989	Felix, Long Melford, 1995
TSV805	MAN 10.180	Berkhof Excellence 1000 Midi	C33F	1991	Chivers, Elstead, 1996
N235WDO	Mercedes-Benz 410D	Autobus Classique	M16	1995	
N245WDO	Mercedes-Benz 410D	Autobus Classique	M16	1995	
N526BFY	Mercedes-Benz 312D	Concept	M12	1996	
P495KAK	Mercedes-Benz 711D	Onyx	C24F	1996	
P331TUM	Mercedes-Benz 412D	Olympus	M13	1997	
P355TUM	Mercedes-Benz 412D	Olympus	M13	1997	
P978HWF	Dennis Javelin SFD531BR3TGJ6	Auwaerter Transliner	C49FT	1997	

Previous Registrations:-

A17ESC	E241MMM	**EX9242**	F600TLB, WET880
137ASV	JTM112V	**TSV805**	H104GKR, H7KFC

Livery:- White with silver, blue and red relief.

ESSEX COACHWAYS

Essex Coachways Ltd, Lode Star House, Watts Grove, Bow, London, E3 3RE

					Previous Owner
HIL9271	Volvo B10M-61	Plaxton Paramount 3200	C53F	1983	Brentwood Coaches, Little Waltham,1995
TMD292Y	Volvo B10M-61	Plaxton Paramount 3200	C32FT	1983	
ADC768A	Volvo B10M-61	Van Hool Alizee H	C53F	1985	Ross, Wrexham, 1994
D256HFX	Volvo B10M-61	Plaxton Paramount 3200 III	C57F	1987	Pathfinder, Chadwell Heath, 1997
F467MAA	Volvo B10M-61	Van Hool Alizee H	C49FT	1988	Pathfinder, Chadwell Heath, 1997
F497UPD	Mercedes-Benz 811D	Reeve Burgess Beaver	C33F	1989	Pathfinder, Chadwell Heath, 1997
2588SX	Volvo B10M-60	Van Hool Alizee SH	C49FT	1990	
H92CJU	Volvo B10M-60	Van Hool Alizee H	C51FT	1990	Pathfinder, Chadwell Heath, 1997
J263JNS	Volvo B10M-60	Van Hool Alizee H	C53F	1992	Crawford, Neilston, 1995
L970KDT	Volvo B10M-60	Van Hool Alizee HE	C32FT	1993	
L265VUS	Volvo B10M-60	Van Hool Alizee HE	C53F	1994	Crawford, Neilston, 1997

Previous Registrations:-

F467MAA	F451WFX, AYU776 (Belgium), XEL606	**F497UPD**	F485WFX, KXI599	**HIL9271**	FUA390Y, 999BWC, UJN215Y

Livery:- Mustard with white and black relief.

FALCON TRAVEL

A.J. Risby & R.E. Baldwin, Unit 4, 123 Nutty Lane, Shepperton, Surrey, TW17 0RQ

					Previous Owner
KBH846V	Leyland Leopard PSU3E/4R	Plaxton Supreme IV	C53F	1980	Frames Rickards, Brentford, 1986
NUT16W	Leyland Leopard PSU3F/5R	Duple Dominant II	C53F	1981	Fylde Transport, 1997
TSU606	Kassbohrer Setra S215HD	Kassbohrer Tornado	C48FT	1985	Birds, North Hykeham, 1994
YXI3056	Volvo B10M-61	Van Hool Alizee H	C53F	1989	Shearings,1996
BAZ7055	Volvo B10M-60	Van Hool Alizee H	C53F	1990	Shearings,1996

Previous Registrations:- **BAZ7055** G855RNC   **TSU606**   6097EL, C356JHE   **YXI3056** F734ENE

Livery:- White with burgundy and black relief.

FERNLEAF COACHES

K.J. & L.A.M. Leigh, 12 Martin Grove, Morden, Surrey, SM4 5AJ

					Previous Owner
B496CBD	Scania K112CRS	Jonckheere Jubilee P599	C51FT	1985	Smith, Wouldham, 1993
F917YNV	Volvo B10M-60	Jonckheere Deauville P599	C49FT	1989	Angel Motors, Tottenham, 1997
H51VNH	Volvo B10M-60	Jonckheere Deauville P599	C51FT	1990	Marchwood, Totton, 1996
K470PNR	Toyota Coaster HDB30R	Caetano Optimo II	C18F	1992	Mears, Thornwood Common, 1997
P849ADO	Mercedes-Benz Sprinter 412D	Autobus Classique	M16	1997	
P221OLC	Mercedes-Benz Sprinter 412D	Autobus Classique	M16	1997	

Livery:- White with green relief.   H51VNH carries logos for London Broncos Team Coach.

FIVEWAYS TRAVEL

C.R. Rich, 516 Purley Way, Croydon, Surrey, CR0 4RE

					Previous Owner
JPE605V	Volvo B58-56	Plaxton Supreme IV	C53F	1980	Hookway, Caterham, 1995
UJI8217	DAF SB3000DHTD585	Plaxton Paramount 3200	C53F	1984	Edwards, Edmonton, 1990
PJI3540	DAF SB2300DHS585	Plaxton Paramount 3200 II	C53F	1985	Barry's, Moreton-in-Marsh, 1997
UJI8216	DAF SB2300DHS585	Plaxton Paramount 3200 II LS	C53F	1985	Evan, Carmarthen, 1997
D560HHA	Ford Transit	Ford	M4L	1987	private owner, 1996
D764LEL	Ford Transit	Ford	M14	1987	private owner, 1996
E995LAE	Ford Transit	Ford	B6FL	1988	private owner, 1996
G973APY	Ford Transit	Ford	M12	1991	Sun Alliance, Bristol, 1996

Previous Registrations:- **PJI3540** B698OBC   **UJI8216** B665OFP   **UJI8217** A877PJX

Livery:- White with red and mauve relief.

FINCHLEY COACHES/SOUTHGATE COACHES

Finchley & Southgate Coaches Ltd, 52 Brunswick Park Road, New Southgate, London, N11 1HA   *Previous Owner*

Finchley Fleet:-

BTX36V	Ford R1114	Plaxton Supreme IV	C53F	1979	Cleverly, Cwmbran, 1982
BTX37V	Ford R1114	Plaxton Supreme IV	C53F	1979	Bailey, Hucknall, 1987
NDG585W	Ford R1114	Duple Dominant II	C53F	1980	Perrett, Shipton Oliffe, 1985
BYJ575Y	Leyland Tiger TRCTL11/3R	Plaxton Paramount 3500	C53F	1983	Plumpton, Plumpton Green, 1989
A213DPB	Leyland Tiger TRCTL11/3RH	Plaxton Paramount 3200 Express	C51F	1983	Wycombe Bus, 1994
A184OEL	Leyland Tiger TRCTL11/3R	Plaxton Paramount 3500	C51F	1984	Yellow Coaches, Bournemouth, 1995
A802XEP	Leyland Tiger TRCTL11/3R	LAG Galaxy	C53F	1984	Davies, Pencader, 1989
B454AAT	Leyland Tiger TRCTL11/3RH	Plaxton Paramount 3500 II	C53F	1985	Yellow Coaches, Bournemouth, 1995
D146HML	Leyland Tiger TRCTL11/3RZ	Duple 320	C53F	1987	Pan Atlas, Acton, 1988
D588MVR	Leyland Tiger TRCTL11/3RZ	Plaxton Paramount 3200 III LS	C53F	1987	Thamesway, 1995
D596MVR	Leyland Tiger TRCTL11/3RZ	Plaxton Paramount 3200 III LS	C53F	1987	Thamesway, 1995

Southgate Fleet:-

BTX38V	Ford R1114	Plaxton Supreme IV	C53F	1979	Cleverly, Cwmbran, 1982
BTX40V	Ford R1114	Plaxton Supreme IV	C53F	1979	Rayleigh, Ramsden Heath, 1987
OHA517W	Ford R1114	Duple Dominant II	C53F	1980	Heart of England, Water Orton, 1987
OHP8W	Ford R1114	Plaxton Supreme IV	C53F	1980	Shaw, Bedworth, 1985
JSV454	Leyland Tiger TRCTL11/3R	Plaxton Paramount 3500	C55F	1983	Armchair, Brentford, 1988
FRU675Y	Leyland Tiger TRCTL11/3R	Plaxton Paramount 3500	C50F	1983	Yellow Coaches, Bournemouth, 1995
UTN955Y	Leyland Tiger TRCTL11/3R	Plaxton Paramount 3500	C51F	1983	Skew, New Milton, 1988
A119PBW	Leyland Tiger TRCTL11/3RH	Plaxton Paramount 3500 Express	C53F	1984	Oxford Bus, 1995
B275AMG	Leyland Tiger TRCTL11/3R	Plaxton Paramount 3200	C53F	1985	Finchley Coaches, 1989
D590MVR	Leyland Tiger TRCTL11/3RZ	Plaxton Paramount 3200 III LS	C53F	1987	Thamesway, 1995
D601MVR	Leyland Tiger TRCTL11/3RZ	Plaxton Paramount 3200 III LS	C53F	1987	Thamesway, 1995

Previous Registrations:-

A184OEL	A993LLJ, RIB8743	**FRU675Y**	KGS490Y, RIB3744	**JSV454** FNM864Y
BYJ575Y	YFG391Y, WSV504			

Livery:- Yellow with orange and blue relief.

FOREST

Questcliffe Ltd, The Coach House, Nelson Street, East Ham, London, E6 2QA

Previous Owner

C519KFL	Leyland Royal Tiger RTC	Leyland Doyen	C53F	1985	Premier, Cambridge, 1989
G478SYS	Hestair-Duple 425 SDA1512	Duple 425	C53FT	1990	Shire, St Albans, 1996
H82FBY	Mercedes-Benz 814L	North West C.S. Buffalo	C35F	1990	private owner, 1996
N185OUT	Iveco Daily 49-10	Iveco	C19F	1996	
P685BEC	Mercedes-Benz 609D	Olympus	C24F	1996	
P837RYR	Iveco ECO3.CC.95	Indcar 80	C35F	1997	

Livery:- White with two tone green relief.

FORESTDALE

Forestdale Coaches Ltd, 45 Holmbury Grove, Featherbed Lane, Forestdale, Croydon, Surrey, CR0 9AP

N1FOR	Bova FHD12-340	Bova Futura	C49FT	1995

Livery:- Red with gold fleetname.

FRAMES RICKARDS

Frames Rickards Ltd, 11 Herbrand Street, Bloomsbury, London, WC1N 1EX

Previous Owner

A1FRX	Volvo B10M-60	Plaxton Paramount 3200 III LS	C50F	1989	Wallace Arnold, 1993
A2FRX	Volvo B10M-60	Plaxton Paramount 3200 III LS	C50F	1989	Wallace Arnold, 1993
A3FRX	Volvo B10M-60	Plaxton Paramount 3200 III LS	C50F	1989	Wallace Arnold, 1993
A4FRX	Volvo B10M-60	Plaxton Paramount 3200 III	C53F	1990	
A5FRX	Volvo B10M-60	Plaxton Paramount 3200 III	C53F	1990	
A6FRX	Volvo B10M-60	Plaxton Paramount 3200 III	C53F	1990	
A9FRX	Scania K93CRB	Plaxton Paramount 3200 III LS	C53F	1991	Shearings, 1994
A10FRX	Scania K93CRB	Plaxton Paramount 3200 III LS	C53F	1991	Shearings, 1994
A7FRX	Scania K93CRB	Plaxton Paramount 3200 III LS	C53F	1991	Shearings, 1994
A8FRX	Scania K93CRB	Plaxton Paramount 3200 III LS	C53F	1991	Shearings, 1994
A11FRX	Scania K113CRB	Plaxton Premiere 320	C53F	1992	Excelsior, Bournemouth, 1994
A13FRX	Scania K113CRB	Plaxton Premiere 320	C53F	1992	Excelsior, Bournemouth, 1994
A12FRX	Scania K113CRB	Plaxton Premiere 320	C53F	1992	Excelsior, Bournemouth, 1994
A14FRX	Volvo B10M-62	Plaxton Premiere 320	C53F	1995	
A15FRX	Volvo B10M-62	Plaxton Premiere 320	C53F	1995	

Previous Registrations:-

A1FRX	F422DUG	**A5FRX**	G648WMG	**A9FRX**	H922DRJ	**A13FRX**	A12XEL, J759YHO
A2FRX	F423DUG	**A6FRX**	G649WMG	**A10FRX**	H925DRJ	**A14FRX**	M428WAK
A3FRX	F433DUG	**A7FRX**	H524DVM	**A11FRX**	A14XEL, J757YHO	**A15FRX**	M429WAK
A4FRX	G647WMG	**A8FRX**	H528DVM	**A12FRX**	A13XEL, J758YHO		

Livery:-   Maroon and black with gold signwriting.   Special Liveries:- British Airways Holidays (Blue and grey with red relief):- A5FRX, A6FRX.

GMV

G.M. Vanstone, 2 Masefield Court, Poets Road, Canonbury, London, N5 2SJ   *Previous Owner*

OYV203T	Ford R1114	Plaxton Supreme III Express	C53F	1978	Stephenson, Easingwold, 1996
HPH713V	Volvo B58-56	Duple Dominant II	C53F	1980	Stonebridge, Biggleswade, 1997
GIL6096	Ford R1114	Plaxton Supreme VI	C53F	1982	Burke, Barking, 1991
A249ODY	Mercedes-Benz L207D	Coachcraft	M12	1983	K. & T., Stratford, 1995
A185UJD	Volvo B10M-56	Plaxton Paramount 3200	C53F	1984	Belsey, Pulborough, 1996
HIB7439	Mercedes-Benz L608D	Coachcraft	C19F	1984	Allen, Hitchin, 1994
GIL4403	Volvo B10M-61	Plaxton Paramount 3200 II	C53F	1986	Shearings, 1994
GBZ3421	Toyota Coaster BB30R	Caetano Optimo	C19F	1987	Bonner, Ongar, 1994

Previous Registrations:-

A249ODY	A605TGO, 9415AP	**GIL4403**	C351DND	**HIB7439**	B530KPH
GBZ3421	D131KMM	**GIL6096**	YDH138X		

Livery:- Cream and red.

G & C TOURS

F. Garcia, 314 Kilburn Lane, Queens Park, London, W9 3EF

M146KJF	Toyota Coaster HZB50R	Caetano Optimo III	C18F	1995
N133RJF	Volvo B10M-62	Plaxton Premiere 320	C57F	1996
P231AUT	Volvo B10M-62	Plaxton Premiere 320	C57F	1997
P233AUT	Volvo B10M-62	Plaxton Premiere 350	C55F	1997
P384GJM	Dennis Javelin	Berkhof Axial	C43F	1997
P646SBD	Mercedes-Benz Sprinter 412D	Mercedes-Benz	M12	1997

Livery:- Light blue with dark blue relief.   P233AUT carries all over advert for Kuoni Helvetic Tours including contravision windows.

GN COACHES

G. Negrotti, 47 Middleton Avenue, Greenford, Middlesex, UB6 8BG

N104BHL	Volvo B10M-62	Plaxton Premiere 350	C53F	1995
P32KWA	Volvo B10M-62	Plaxton Premiere 350	C53F	1997

Livery:- White.

GAYTIME

D.J. & I.M. Lock, 48 Vera Road, Fulham, London, SW6 6QW

					Previous Owner
TSV760	Scania K112CRS	Van Hool Alizee H	C49FT	1986	BCP, Gatwick, 1988
F389RML	Van Hool T815	Van Hool Alicron	C53F	1989	
J409AWF	Volvo B10M-60	Van Hool Alizee H	C48FT	1992	Tellings-Golden Miller, Byfleet, 1987

Previous Registration:- **TSV760** C242THC

Livery:- Grey and silver with white and blue relief.

GOLDENSTAND

Goldenstand Coaches Ltd, 15 Chase Road, North Acton, London, NW10 6PT

					Previous Owner
UKE503R	Ford R1114	Duple Dominant II	C53F	1976	Bevan, Bournemouth, 1996
WRJ212S	Ford R1114	Plaxton Supreme III	C53F	1978	Hudson, Rowlands Castle, 1995
CAX16V	Ford R1114	Plaxton Supreme IV	C41DL	1980	Scott, Peckham,1986
DHV479W	Leyland Leopard PSU5C/4R	Duple Dominant II	C57F	1980	Whitehead, Bournemouth, 1996
ODJ596W	Ford R1114	Duple Dominant II	C53F	1981	Gelsthorpe, Mansfield, 1995
ACH72A	MAN SR280	MAN	C49FT	1981	Rochester, Boscombe, 1995
IIL9408	Scania K112CRS	Jonckheere Jubilee P599	C57F	1984	Derek Randall, North Acton, 1985
A72JOY	Iveco 35F8	Robin Hood	M12	1984	
A75JOY	Iveco 35F8	Robin Hood	M12	1984	
CIL8589	DAF SB2300DHS585	Plaxton Paramount 3200	C53F	1984	
IIL6265	Scania K112CRS	Jonckheere Jubilee P50	C51FT	1984	Cantabrica, Watford, 1989
IIL6906	Scania K112CRS	Jonckheere Jubilee P50	C53F	1984	Crawford, Neilston, 1989
B595LJU	DAF MB200DKFL600	LAG Galaxy	C49FT	1984	Ayres, Dalkeith, 1995
B876EOM	Ford Transit	Robin Hood	M12	1985	private owner, 1986
B813JPN	Leyland Tiger TRCTL11/3R	Duple Caribbean II	C55F	1985	Williams, Porthcawl, 1995
C984YFA	DAF MB200DKFL600	Duple Caribbean II	C53F	1985	Staffordian, Stafford, 1994
D775LUG	Freight-Rover Sherpa	Optare	M16	1987	Maybury, Verwood, 1994
K354CRD	Leyland-DAF 400	Pearl	M16	1993	
L453FTF	Leyland-DAF 400	Goldenstand	M16	1993	
L403GMO	LDV 400	Goldenstand	M8L	1993	
M854NCF	LDV 400	Goldenstand	M16	1994	
M721XOT	LDV 400	Goldenstand	M8L	1994	
M722XOT	LDV 400	Goldenstand	M16	1995	

Previous Registrations:-

ACH72A NFJ372W, 2779UE, PWL811W
C984YFA C759UVT, MIB581
CIL8589 A229LFX
IIL6265 A598XRP
IIL6906 B511GBD
IIL9408 A63JLW
UKE503R PKX262R, EUI1587

Livery:- White with red relief and black signwriting.

GOLDEN TOURS

Golden Tours Ltd, Unit 4 Fountain Square, 123-151 Buckingham Palace Road, Victoria, London, SW1 9SH

M238EOU	LDV 400	LDV	M9	1995
M239EOU	LDV 400	LDV	M9	1995
M101FGP	Mercedes-Benz 410D	Crystals	M16	1995
M102FGP	Mercedes-Benz 410D	Crystals	M16	1995
N582AWJ	Dennis Javelin 12SDA2166	Auwaerter Transliner	C49FT	1996
N294LGH	LDV 400	Euromotive	M16	1996
N295LGH	LDV 400	Euromotive	M16	1996
N39MGJ	LDV 400	Euromotive	M16	1996
P968HWF	Dennis Javelin 531BR3TGJ6	Auwaerter Transliner	C49FT	1996
P381MLU	Volkswagen Caravelle TDI	Volkswagen	M7	1996

Livery:- White with blue, red and yellow relief.

A. GREEN OF LONDON

A. Green (Coaches) Ltd, 357a Hoe Street, Walthamstow, London, E17 9AP

					Previous Owner
THR752	Volvo B10M-61	Plaxton Paramount 3500	C53F	1984	Ralph's, Langley, 1992
F967WFA	Volvo B10M-60	Plaxton Paramount 3500 III	C51FT	1989	Baker, Biddulph, 1996
G956VBC	DAF SB2305DHS585	Caetano Algarve	C49FT	1990	
G957VBC	DAF SB2305DHS585	Caetano Algarve	C53F	1990	
N237NNR	Volvo B10M-62	Caetano Algarve II	C49FT	1995	

Previous Registrations:-

F967WFA   8399RU   **THR752**   A700XMH

Livery:- White with orange and yellow relief.

GREY-GREEN

T. Cowie plc, 53-55 Stamford Hill, London, N16 5TD

895	E895KYW	Scania K92CRB	Van Hool Alizee H	C53F	1988
896	E896KYW	Scania K92CRB	Van Hool Alizee H	C53F	1988
897	E897KYW	Scania K92CRB	Van Hool Alizee H	C53F	1988
898	E898KYW	Scania K92CRB	Van Hool Alizee H	C53F	1988
905	G905TYR	DAF MB230LB615	Van Hool Alizee H	C53F	1990
906	G906TYR	DAF MB230LB615	Van Hool Alizee H	C53F	1990
907	G907TYR	DAF MB230LB615	Van Hool Alizee H	C53F	1990
908	G908TYR	DAF MB230LB615	Van Hool Alizee H	C49FT	1990
909	G909TYR	DAF MB230LB615	Van Hool Alizee H	C49FT	1990
910	G910TYR	DAF MB230LB615	Van Hool Alizee H	C49FT	1990
932	K932VCP	DAF MB230LTF615	Van Hool Alizee HE	C49FT	1993
933	K933VCP	DAF MB230LTF615	Van Hool Alizee HE	C49FT	1993

942-947		DAF SB3000WS601	Van Hool Alizee HE	C49FT	1994 (944-947 are 1995)

942	M942LYR	943	M943LYR	944	M944LYR	945	M945LYR	946	M946LYR	947	M947LYR

948	M948LYR	DAF SB3000WS601	Van Hool Alizee HE	C53F	1995
949	M949LYR	DAF SB3000WS601	Van Hool Alizee HE	C53F	1995

The bus fleet is listed in the *London Bus Handbook*.

Livery:-   White with green and orange relief.   Special Liveries Eurolines (White) :- 932, 933, 942-947

GUIDELINE

Guideline Coaches Ltd, 73 Woodmansterne Road, Streatham Vale, London, SW16 5UU   *Previous Owner*

DBZ945	Mercedes-Benz 0303/15R	Mercedes-Benz	C49FT	1986	Yeates, Loughborough (Demonstrator), 1987
929ECH	Toyota Coaster HDB30R	Caetano Optimo II	C21F	1992	The Kings Ferry, Gillingham, 1995
M255JBC	Toyota Coaster HZB50R	Caetano Optimo III	C21F	1994	Gaytime, Fulham, 1997

Previous Registrations:- **DBZ945** D757XBC   **929ECH** K212SFP, K13KFC, K651VKN

Livery:- Two tone blue and white.

HAMILTON

D.L. Bennett, 589-591 Uxbridge Road, Hayes End, Middlesex, UB4 8HP   *Previous Owner*

A7HOU	DAF MB200DKFL600	Van Hool Alizee H	C50FT	1984	Knight, Sidcup, 1994
KLP1D	Bedford VAS5	Duple Dominant	C16F	1985	Royal Household, 1996
A4HOU	Kassbohrer Setra S215HD	Kassbohrer Tornado	C49FT	1986	Cavalier, West Molesey, 1993
A6HOU	Leyland Royal Tiger RTC	Leyland Doyen	C49FT	1987	Copeland, Mier, 1995
D794SNB	Ford R1014	Plaxton Paramount 3200 II	C35F	1987	Bullock, Cheadle, 1997
E589CFW	Mercedes-Benz 507D	Mercedes-Benz	C16F	1988	private owner, 1995
F69SMC	Mercedes-Benz 811D	Reeve Burgess Beaver	C25F	1988	London Borough of Harrow, 1993
G472GNH	DAF SB2305DHS585	Jonckheere Deauville P599	C51FT	1989	Hurst & Leak, Goose Green, 1996
A3FTG	Volvo B10M-53	Plaxton Paramount 4000RS III	CH55/12DT	1990	Flights, Birmingham, 1997
A4FTG	Volvo B10M-53	Plaxton Paramount 4000RS III	CH49/12DT	1990	Flights, Birmingham, 1997
K35PLO	Sanos S315.21	FAP Charisma	C47FT	1992	
M706HBC	Dennis Javelin 12SDA2136	Marcopolo Explorer	C51FT	1995	
M709HBC	Dennis Javelin 12SDA2136	Marcopolo Explorer	C51FT	1995	
N801SJU	Dennis Javelin 12SDA2170	Marcopolo Explorer	C51FT	1996	
N802SJU	Dennis Javelin 12SDA2170	Marcopolo Explorer	C51FT	1996	

Previous Registrations:-

A3FTG	G717JOG
A4FTG	G727JOG, FTG9
A4HOU	D804XPJ
A6HOU	D813SET, MIB502
A7HOU	B360DWF, WOI504, WSV488, B940MKP
D794SNB	D391BNR, BUI1300

Livery:- Various.

HAMPTON'S OF LONDON

Hampton Coaches (Westminster) Ltd, 54b Trundleys Road, Deptford, London, SE8 5JG
A.T. Cocklin, 54b Trundleys Road, Deptford, London, SE8 5JG
Lock's Coaches, 54b Trundleys Road, Deptford, London SE8 5JG

Previous Owner

XEX160S	Bedford VAS5	Plaxton Supreme III	C29F	1978	Norfolk Motor Services, Great Yarmouth, 1980
EWW221T	Leyland Leopard PSU3E/4R	Duple Dominant II	C53F	1979	Cocklin, Deptford, 1994
YPL81T	AEC Reliance 6U2R	Duple Dominant II Express	C49F	1979	Poulton, South Bermondsey, 1994
MYX32X	Bedford YNT	Duple Dominant II	C53F	1982	Golden Travel, North Kensington, 1988
UYA699	Volvo B10M-61	Duple Goldliner IV	C51FT	1982	Tentrek, Sidcup, 1987
YMA696	Volvo B10M-61	Plaxton Paramount 3500	C51FT	1984	Transcity, Sidcup, 1989
A77JWD	Ford R1115	Duple Dominant IV	C53F	1984	Bennett, Gloucester, 1986
119UYA	Bedford YNT	Plaxton Paramount 3200 II	C53F	1985	Willetts, Yorkley, 1991
SJI2954	Leyland Tiger TRCTL11/3R	LAG Galaxy	C53F	1985	Osborne, Tollesbury, 1997

Previous Registrations:-

MYX32X 248D240	**SJI2954** B444BAR	**119UYA** B105PJF	**UYA699** VGU907X	**YMA696** A764HGX

Livery:- Blue

HARDINGS

D.J. & J.S. Harding, Wellwood, Wellhouse Lane, Betchworth, Surrey, RH3 7HH

Previous Owner

HCT554	Kassbohrer Setra S215HR	Kassbohrer Rational	C53F	1984	Premier-Albanian, Watford, 1985
NSU496	Volvo B10M-61	Van Hool Alizee H	C53F	1985	Shearings, 1990
NSU137	Volvo B10M-61	Van Hool Alizee H	C53F	1986	Shearings, 1991
E989NMK	Mercedes-Benz 609D	Reeve Burgess Beaver	C25F	1988	
E589VTH	Volvo B10M-61	Plaxton Paramount 3500 III	C53F	1988	Shearings, 1990
F468SPH	Mercedes-Benz 811D	Reeve Burgess Beaver	C25F	1989	
G884VNA	Scania K93CRB	Plaxton Paramount 3200 III	C53F	1990	Lowland, 1996
L2HCT	Mercedes-Benz 711D	Plaxton Beaver	C25F	1994	
M5HCT	Volvo B10M-62	Jonckheere Deauville 45	C51FT	1995	
N3HCT	Toyota Coaster HZB50R	Caetano Optimo III	C21F	1995	
N4HCT	Scania K113CRB	Van Hool Alizee HE	C53F	1996	

Previous Registrations :- **HCT554** A246GPL   **NSU496** B479UNB   **E589VTH** E589VTH, NSU137   **NSU137** C527DND

Livery:- White with red and orange relief.

HAROLD WOOD COACHES

F.W. Leach, 12 Woodlands Road, Harold Wood, Essex, RM3 0QX

HIL7197	Bedford YLQ	Plaxton Supreme IV	C45F	1979
HIL7196	Bedford YLQ	Plaxton Supreme IV	C45F	1980
HIL7195	Bedford YLQ	Plaxton Supreme IV	C45F	1981
VJI1151	Leyland Tiger TRCTL11/3RZ	Plaxton Paramount 3500 II	C57F	1985
VJI1152	Leyland Tiger TRCTL11/3RZ	Plaxton Paramount 3500 II	C53F	1985
VJI1153	Volvo B10M-61	Plaxton Paramount 3500 II	C53F	1986
VJI1154	Volvo B10M-61	Plaxton Paramount 3500 II	C53F	1986
G915WAY	Volvo B10M-60	Caetano Algarve	C57F	1990
P50HWC	Volvo B10M-62	Caetano Algarve II	C49FT	1997

Named Vehicles:-

VJI1153	Euro I	P50HWC	Euro IV	G915WAY	Euro VII
VJI1154	Euro II	VJI1152	Euro V		

Previous Registrations:-

HIL7195	HMU425W	**HIL7197**	CMJ460T	**VJI1152**	C391DML	**VJI1154**	D124HMH
HIL7196	CMT919V	**VJI1151**	B291AMG	**VJI1153**	D123HMH		

Livery:- Cream with orange and two tone blue relief.

HEARN'S

R. Hearn, 801 Kenton Lane, Harrow, Middlesex, HA3 6AH

Previous Owner

HIL5876	Leyland Leopard PSU3C/4R	Plaxton Supreme III	C51F	1978	
HIL2153	Leyland Leopard PSU5C/4R	Plaxton Supreme IV	C57F	1979	
HIL2154	Leyland Leopard PSU5C/4R	Plaxton Supreme IV	C57F	1979	
GDP266V	Bedford YMT	Plaxton Supreme IV Express	C53F	1980	Owen, Yateley, 1996
HIL2156	Leyland Leopard PSU3E/4R	Plaxton Supreme IV	C53F	1980	
HIL2155	Leyland Leopard PSU3E/4R	Plaxton Supreme IV	C53F	1982	
968KUR	Leyland Tiger TRCTL11/2R	Plaxton Supreme V	C53F	1982	Rover, Chesham, 1992
LVG878	Leyland Tiger TRCTL11/3R	Plaxton Paramount 3500	C50F	1983	
HIL2157	Leyland Tiger TRCTL11/3R	Plaxton Paramount 3200	C57F	1984	Ebdon, Sidcup, 1986
HIL2158	Leyland Tiger TRCTL11/3R	Plaxton Paramount 3200	C57F	1984	The Londoners, Nunhead, 1986
HIL2159	Leyland Tiger TRCTL11/3R	Plaxton Paramount 3200 II	C55F	1985	Armchair, Brentford, 1986
HIL2160	Leyland Tiger TRCTL11/3R	Plaxton Paramount 3200 II	C57F	1985	Armchair, Brentford, 1986

B507CGP	Volvo B10M-61	Plaxton Paramount 3200 III	C53F	1985	Epsom Coaches, 1995
C511LGH	Volvo B10M-61	Plaxton Paramount 3200 III	C53F	1986	Epsom Coaches, 1995
EAZ8412	Leyland Tiger TRCTL11/3RZ	Plaxton Paramount 3200 III	C57F	1987	Smith, Sittingbourne, 1995
EAZ8413	Leyland Tiger TRCTL11/3RZ	Plaxton Paramount 3200 III	C57F	1987	Smith, Sittingbourne, 1995
HIL2385	Bedford YNT	Plaxton Paramount 3200 III	C53F	1987	Owen, Yateley, 1993
SJI7046	Bedford YNT	Plaxton Paramount 3200 III	C53F	1987	Owen, Yateley, 1993
SJI7417	Mercedes-Benz 307D	Reeve Burgess	M12	1987	
SJI7415	Leyland Tiger TRCTL11/3ARZ	Plaxton Paramount 3200 III	C55F	1988	Armchair, Brentford, 1993
SJI7416	Leyland Tiger TRCTL11/3ARZ	Plaxton Paramount 3200 III	C55F	1988	Armchair, Brentford, 1993
HIL8518	Leyland Tiger TRCTL11/3ARZ	Plaxton Paramount 3200 III	C57F	1988	
HIL8519	Leyland Tiger TRCTL11/3ARZ	Plaxton Paramount 3200 III	C57F	1988	
JIL7233	Volvo B10M-61	Plaxton Paramount 3200 III	C53F	1988	Keighley & District, 1997
E360NEG	Volvo B10M-61	Plaxton Paramount 3200 III	C53F	1988	Sovereign, 1997
E362NEG	Volvo B10M-61	Plaxton Paramount 3200 III	C53F	1988	Sovereign, 1996
SJI7049	Volvo B10M-60	Plaxton Paramount 3200 III	C53F	1989	Frames Rickards, Bloomsbury, 1994
SJI7054	Volvo B10M-60	Plaxton Paramount 3200 III	C53F	1989	Frames Rickards, Bloomsbury, 1994
G285STT	Leyland Tiger TRCTL10/3ARZM	Plaxton Paramount 3500 III	C53F	1989	Brent's, Watford, 1995

Previous Registrations:-

968KUR	DNK590Y		**HIL2385**	D390BNR
EAZ8412	E75VKO		**HIL5876**	VMJ964S
EAZ8413	E76VKO		**HIL8518**	E318OMG
GDP266V	ECY278V, ONY837		**HIL8519**	E319OMG
HIL2153	GBM122T		**JIL7233**	E367NEG
HIL2154	GBM123T		**LVG878**	A387NNK
HIL2155	ANK315X		**SJI7046**	E829EUT, OVK902, E848KCF
HIL2156	PRO441W		**SJI7049**	F891SMU
HIL2157	A193RUR		**SJI7054**	F889SMU
HIL2158	A194RUR		**SJI7415**	E994NMK
HIL2159	B401CMC		**SJI7416**	E995NMK
HIL2160	B402CMC		**SJI7417**	E42MMT

Livery:- Grey, light blue and white.

HOUSTON & BRYANT

J.R. Houston & L.R. Bryant, Boundary Garage, 38 Crawley Road, Wood Green, London, N22 6AN

						Previous Owner
LUA272V	Leyland Leopard PSU3F/4R	Plaxton Supreme IV	C53F	1980	Cottrell, Mitcheldean, 1989
BBM77A	Volvo B10M-61	Jonckheere Bermuda	C49FT	1981	Renyard, Totton, 1987
YSV738	Leyland Leopard PSU5D/4R	Plaxton Supreme V	C53F	1981	Wessex, 1990
B251AMG	Bedford YNT	Plaxton Paramount 3200	C53F	1984	Angel Motors, Tottenham, 1989
C593VUT	DAF SB2300DHS585	Smit Orion	C53FT	1986	Daniels, Abridge, 1992
E478GBV	Mercedes-Benz 609D	Reeve Burgess	C19F	1987	East Pennine, Halifax, 1990
E38YDO	Mercedes-Benz 609D	Advanced Vehicle Builders	C21F	1988	
F590HUS	Talbot Freeway	Talbot	DP12FL	1989	McDade, Uddingston, 1994
F488VRP	Iveco Daily 49.10	Leicester Carriage Builders	M13L	1989	Northamptonshire County Council, 1993
G346EOK	Leyland-DAF 400	Jubilee	M14L	1990	RNIB, Wembley, 1994
G54GBD	Leyland-DAF 400	Crystals (1993)	M12L	1990	private owner, 1993
G939AAY	Leyland-DAF 400	Walsall Conversions (1994)	M16L	1990	private owner, 1994
H728BRG	Ford Transit	Ford	M8L	1991	private owner 1992
H649COD	Leyland-DAF 400	Zodiac (1993)	M12L	1991	private owner, 1993
H112YSU	Talbot Freeway	Talbot	B16FL	1990	McDade, Uddingston, 1996
H115YSU	Talbot Freeway	Talbot	B16FL	1990	McDade, Uddingston, 1996
H117YSU	Talbot Freeway	Talbot	B16FL	1990	McDade, Uddingston, 1995
J906BUA	Leyland-DAF 400	Crystals	M16	1991	Cropper, Kirkstall, 1994
J180MNX	Talbot Freeway	Talbot	B16FL	1991	Nottingham City Transport, 1995
J448MDB	Leyland-DAF 400	Made To Measure	M16	1992	Holloway, Scunthorpe, 1995
J769NHA	Leyland-DAF 400	Jubilee	M16	1992	Fairway, Hull, 1994
K622WOV	Talbot Freeway	TBP	B18FL	1992	Harris Bus, West Thurrock,1996
K623WOV	Talbot Freeway	TBP	B18FL	1992	Harris Bus, West Thurrock,1996
K676HWC	Leyland-DAF 400	Walsall Conversions (1994)	M16L	1993	private owner, 1994
K183NLV	Leyland-DAF 400	Walsall Conversions (1994)	M16L	1993	private owner, 1994
L764KWL	Leyland-DAF 400	Walsall Conversions	M16L	1994	

Named Vehicle:- YSV738   The Brigadier

Previous Registrations:- **BBM77A**   WNH823W   **YSV738**   SND292X

Livery:- White with yellow and green relief.

HUMMINGBIRD

Hummingbird Enterprises Ltd, 37 Sunray Avenue, Bromley, Kent, BR2 8EN

					Previous Owner
106KUP	Bova FHD12-280	Bova Futura	C49FT	1986	Graham, Camberwell, 1994

Previous Registration:- **106KUP** C50NVK

Livery:- Silver and two tone blue.

IMPACT

A. Hill, 46 Drayton Green Road, West Ealing, London, W13 8RY   *Previous Owner*

Reg	Chassis	Body	Seating	Year	Previous Owner
C567XLK	Ford Transit	Deansgate	M12	1986	Wings, Hayes, 1989
D219NUR	Ford Transit	Chassis Developments	C16F	1986	
ONT46	Volvo B10M-61	Jonkheere Jubilee P599	C51FT	1988	Globeheath, Cardiff, 1991
F135UMD	Leyland Swift LBM6T/2RSO	Reeve Burgess Harrier	C37F	1989	
G652UHU	Mercedes-Benz 609D	Made To Measure	C26F	1989	
JIL3125	MAN 10.180	Caetano Algarve	C35F	1990	Flagfinders, Braintree, 1996
G171XHU	Mercedes-Benz 609D	Made To Measure	C26F	1990	
H187CVU	Mercedes-Benz 609D	Made To Measure	C24F	1990	
H197CVU	Talbot Express	Made To Measure	M8	1990	
H198CVU	Talbot Express	Made To Measure	M8	1990	
H207CVU	Talbot Express	Made To Measure	M12	1990	
H208CVU	Talbot Express	Made To Measure	M12	1990	
H704YUV	Iveco Daily 49-10	Reeve Burgess Beaver	B20FL	1990	London United, 1997
H705YUV	Iveco Daily 49.10	Reeve Burgess Beaver	B20FL	1990	London United, 1997
H708YUV	Iveco Daily 49.10	Reeve Burgess Beaver	B20FL	1990	London United, 1997
GSU382	Volvo B10M-60	Plaxton Paramount 3500 III	C49FT	1991	Moor-Dale, Newcastle,1996
H413DVM	Leyland-DAF 400	Made To Measure	C16F	1991	
H415DVM	Mercedes-Benz 609D	Made To Measure	C24F	1991	
J47NJT	Volvo B10M-60	Plaxton Excalibur	C49FT	1992	Jones, Market Drayton, 1997
L402CND	Leyland-DAF 400	Concept	C16FL	1993	
L551CND	Leyland-DAF 400	Concept	C16F	1993	
L552CND	Leyland-DAF 400	Concept	C16F	1993	
L553CND	Leyland-DAF 400	Concept	C16F	1993	
L554CND	Leyland-DAF 400	Concept	C16F	1993	
L232DNC	Talbot Express	Concept	M12	1993	
L233DNC	Talbot Express	Concept	M12	1993	
L234DNC	Talbot Express	Concept	M12	1993	
L191DNF	Mercedes-Benz 709D	Mellor	DP16C	1993	Budget Rentals, Bedfont, 1997
L192DNF	Mercedes-Benz 709D	Mellor	DP16C	1993	Budget Rentals, Bedfont, 1997
L436CND	Leyland-DAF 400	Concept	C16F	1994	
L195SCM	Mercedes-Benz 609D	Concept	C24F	1994	
M456MNF	Ford Transit	Deansgate	M8	1994	
M457MNF	Ford Transit	Deansgate	M8	1994	
M651NDB	LDV 400	Concept	M16	1994	
M652NDB	LDV 400	Concept	M16	1994	
M407BLC	Volvo B10M-62	Plaxton Excalibur	C53F	1995	
M107OBU	Ford Transit	Deansgate	M8	1995	
M749WCM	Mercedes-Benz 609D	Concept	C24F	1995	

N731CKF	Mercedes-Benz 609D	Concept		C24F	1995	
N665DFY	Mercedes-Benz 609D	Concept		C24F	1996	
N429YNB	LDV 200	Concept		M8	1996	
N299YRJ	LDV 400	Concept		M16	1996	
P479FDB	LDV Pilot	Concept		M8	1996	
P482FDB	LDV Pilot	Concept		M8	1996	
P483FDB	LDV Pilot	Concept		M8	1996	
P594HHF	Mercedes-Benz 611D	Concept		C14FL	1997	
P141MNB	LDV Convoy	Concept		M16	1997	

Previous Registrations:-

GSU382	H660UWR, H658UWR	**C567XLK**	C334DVU, WET342	**J47NJT**	A2XEL
ONT46	E208GNV				

Livery:- White with magenta signwriting.

INTERNATIONAL COACH LINES

International Coach Lines Ltd, 19 Nursery Road, Thornton Heath, Surrey, CR7 8RE   *Previous Owner*

RM259	VLT259	AEC Routemaster R2RH	Park Royal	H36/28R	1960	preservation, 1996
RM471	KVS601	AEC Routemaster R2RH	Park Royal	H36/28R	1960	preservation, 1996
RM1083	XVS850	AEC Routemaster R2RH	Park Royal	H36/28RD	1962	Time Travel, Thornton Heath, 1996
RMF2771	RCN701	AEC Routemaster 3R2RH	Park Royal	H41/31F	1963	Time Travel, Thornton Heath, 1996
RMA52	NMY637E	AEC Routemaster R2RH/2	Park Royal	H32/24F	1967	Time Travel, Thornton Heath, 1996
RMA57	NMY654E	AEC Routemaster R2RH/2	Park Royal	H32/24F	1967	preservation, 1996
	NMC528	Leyland Tiger TRCTL11/3RZ	Duple 320	C50FT	1987	Time Travel, Thornton Heath, 1996
	405UPJ	Volvo B10M-61	Jonckheere Deauville P599	C49FT	1987	Cordery & Matthews, Heathfield, 1997
	SRU925	Volvo B10M-61	Van Hool Alizee H	C49FT	1988	Jacobs, Southampton, 1996
	191TPH	Volvo B10M-61	Jonckheere Deauville P599	C51FT	1988	Time Travel, Thornton Heath, 1996
	YJR248	LDV 400	LDV	M16	1994	Time Travel, Thornton Heath, 1996
	N830DKU	Scania K113TRB	Irizar Century 12.37	C49FT	1996	A & R, Bedfont, 1997
	P398VUY	Ford Transit	Ford	M14	1997	

Previous Registrations:-

KVS601	WLT471, EDS394A	**191TPH**	E503KNV	**XVS850**	83CLT
NMC528	D134HML	**405UPJ**	D33RKX, 898CCH, D742ELH		
SRU925	E616NBP	**YJR248**	M380LJA		

Livery:- Various

ISLEWORTH COACHES

A.C. & D.F. Blackford, 45 Hall Road, Isleworth, Middlesex, TW7 7PA

Previous Owner

PDC159X	Mercedes-Benz L307D	Coachcraft	M12	1982	Price Global, Hounslow, 1995
E167GFA	Mercedes-Benz 609D	North West Coach Sales	C16F	1987	Aron, Northolt, 1997
RJI5720	Volvo B10M-61	Plaxton Paramount 3500 III	C51FT	1989	Rennie, Dunfermline, 1997
4426BY	Volvo B10M-61	Plaxton Paramount 3500 III	C51FT	1989	Rennie, Dunfermline, 1997

Previous Registrations:- **RJI5720** G170LET   **4426BY** F805COJ, 191WHW, F835FOS, IIW8815

Liveries:- Dark blue (PDC159X), light blue (E167GFA) or blue and red with white relief (RJI5720 and 4426BY)

KENTISHMEN

K.B. Chisholm, 26 Wisteria Gardens, Swanley, Kent, BR9 7TX

Previous Owner

TIB9216	Volvo B58-61	Plaxton Supreme IV	C52FT	1980	A Line, Bedworth, 1994
CIB926	Kassbohrer Setra S215HR	Kassbohrer Rational	C53F	1986	Capital, West Drayton, 1991
CIB8867	Kassbohrer Setra S215HD	Kassbohrer Tornado	C49FT	1988	
CIB3683	Kassbohrer Setra S215HR	Kassbohrer Rational	C53F	1990	Silver Coach Lines, Edinburgh, 1993
CIB331	Auwaerter Neoplan N122/3	Auwaerter Skyliner	CH57/20CT	1990	Trathens, Plymouth, 1995

Previous Registrations:-

CIB331	H201AOD	**CIB8867**	E761JPM
CIB926	2212MW, 8628MW, 2212MW, 1093MW, C384XLL	**TIB9216**	DTY351W, AEF470A, TVC516W
CIB3683	G50HDW		

Named Vehicles:-

CIB331	Dover Castle	CIB3683	Scotney Castle	TIB9216	Chilham Castle
CIB926	Allington Castle	CIB8867	Rochester Castle		

Livery:- Dark blue with light blue relief.

THE KINGS FERRY

The Kings Ferry Ltd, The Coach Station, Pump Lane, Lower Rainham, Gillingham, Kent, ME8 7TJ   *Previous Owner*

2.2	M9KFC	Toyota Coaster HZB50R	Caetano Optimo III	C21F	1995	
2.3	M10KFC	Toyota Coaster HZB50R	Caetano Optimo III	C21F	1995	
3.1	M3KFC	MAN 11.190HOCLR	Berkhof Excellence 1000 Midi	C33FT	1994	
3.4	L4KFC	MAN 11.190HOCLR	Berkhof Excellence 1000 Midi	C33FT	1993	
3.5	PSU699	Kassbohrer Setra S210HD	Kassbohrer Optimal	C35FT	1990	Smith, Marple, 1994
4.1	GIL8490	Mercedes-Benz 0303/15	Mercedes-Benz	C49FT	1988	Scarlet Band, West Cornforth, 1991

4.2-4.6		Mercedes-Benz 0303/2	Mercedes-Benz	C49FT	1991

4.2	H2KFC	4.3	H3KFC	4.4	H4KFC	4.5	H5KFC	4.6	H6KFC

4.7	RJI2713	Kassbohrer Setra S215HD	Kassbohrer Tornado	C49FT	1990	Hallmark, Luton, 1994
4.8	RJI2714	Kassbohrer Setra S215HD	Kassbohrer Tornado	C49FT	1990	Hallmark, Luton, 1994
4.9	K5KFC	Scania K113CRB	Berkhof Excellence 2000HL	C49FT	1993	
4.10	H13KFC	Auwaerter Neoplan N116/3	Auwaerter Cityliner	C48FT	1990	Parry, Cheslyn Hay, 1994
4.11	K6KFC	Scania K113CRB	Berkhof Excellence 2000	C49FT	1993	
4.12	J4KFC	Scania K113CRB	Berkhof Excellence 2000	C49FT	1992	
4.13	J5KFC	Scania K113CRB	Berkhof Excellence 2000	C49FT	1992	
4.14	J6KFC	Scania K113CRB	Berkhof Excellence 2000	C49FT	1992	
4.15	M17KFC	Scania K113CRB	Irizar Century 12.37	C51FT	1997	
4.16	M18KFC	Scania K113TRB	Irizar Century 12.37	C51FT	1997	
4.17	M19KFC	Scania K113CRB	Irizar Century 12.37	C51FT	1997	
4.18	P983LKL	Scania K113CRB	Irizar Century 12.35	C49FT	1997	
4.19	K7KFC	Scania K113CRB	Berkhof Excellence 2000	C49FT	1993	
4.20	K8KFC	Scania K113CRB	Berkhof Excellence 2000	C49FT	1993	
4.21	H11KFC	Auwaerter Neoplan N116/3	Auwaerter Cityliner	C49FT	1990	Happy Days, Woodseaves, 1993
4.22	L8KFC	Bova FHD12.340	Bova Futura	C51FT	1994	
4.23	M2KFC	Scania K113CRB	Irizar Century 12.35	C49FT	1994	
4.27	P984LKL	Scania K113CRB	Irizar Century 12.35	C49FT	1997	
4.28	P985LKL	Scania K113TRB	Irizar Century 12.37	C51FT	1997	
4.29	P986LKL	Scania K113TRB	Irizar Century 12.37	C51FT	1997	
5.1	P661LKO	Scania K113CRB	Van Hool Alizee HE	C53F	1997	
5.2	P802MKL	Scania K113CRB	Van Hool Alizee HE	C53F	1997	
5.3	P803MKL	Scania K113CRB	Van Hool Alizee HE	C53F	1997	
5.4	P804MKL	Scania K113CRB	Van Hool Alizee HE	C53F	1997	
5.5	P805MKL	Scania K113CRB	Van Hool Alizee HE	C53F	1997	
5.6	L6KFC	Bova FHD12.340	Bova Futura	C55F	1994	
5.7	L7KFC	Bova FHD12.340	Bova Futura	C55F	1994	
5.11	H20KFC	Mercedes-Benz 0303	Plaxton Paramount 3500 III	C53F	1991	

5.14	J7KFC	Mercedes-Benz 0303	Plaxton Paramount 3500 III	C53F	1992	
5.15	J8KFC	Mercedes-Benz 0303	Plaxton Paramount 3500 III	C53F	1992	
7.1	K14KFC	Scania K113TRB	Berkhof Excellence 3000HD	CH57/19CT	1993	
7.2	K15KFC	Scania K113TRB	Berkhof Excellence 3000HD	CH57/19CT	1993	
7.3	L5KFC	Scania K113TRA	Berkhof Excellence 3000HD	CH57/23CT	1994	
7.4	M4KFC	Scania K113TRA	Berkhof Excellence 3000HD	CH57/23CT	1994	
7.5	L3KFC	Auwaerter Neoplan N122/3	Auwaerter Skyliner	CH57/20CT	1994	Peter Carol, Bristol, 1997

Previous Registrations:-

| GIL8490 | E989KJF | | RJI2714 | G507YFE | | H13KFC | H155RHE |
| RJI2713 | G506YFE | | H11KFC | H652NFA, H811HVT, BVA300 | | L3KFC | L967MWB, TJI6923. |

Livery:- Primrose with three tone green relief.

KNIGHTS

J.V.H. Knight, The Coach Station, Wren Road, Sidcup, Kent, DA14 4NA   *Previous Owner*

GIL2774	DAF MB200DKFL600	LAG Galaxy	C53F	1983	Grand Tours, Sandown, 1997
WSV486	Bova FHD12-290	Bova Futura	C53F	1986	Longthornton, Surrey Docks, 1991
WSV485	Bova FHD12-290	Bova Futura	C49FT	1989	Richards & Webb, Andover, 1994

Previous Registrations:- **GIL2774** BFP904Y   **WSV485** F259NUT   **WSV486** LSV830

Liveries:- Various

LACEY'S

Lacey's (East Ham) Ltd, 222 Barking Road, East Ham, London, E6 3BB   *Previous Owner*

RIB1736	Leyland Leopard PSU5C/4R	Plaxton Supreme IV	C53F	1979	
RIB1737	Leyland Leopard PSU5C/4R	Plaxton Supreme IV	C53F	1980	
PRO444W	Volvo B58-61	Plaxton Supreme IV	C34FT	1980	
UHM79	Volvo B10M-61	Plaxton Supreme IV	C53F	1981	
LIL4348	Leyland Tiger TRCTL11/3R	Plaxton Paramount 3500	C55F	1984	Cavalier, Hounslow, 1985
LIL2836	Leyland Royal Tiger B50	Van Hool Alizee SH	C49FT	1985	
C901FMP	Leyland Tiger TRCTL11/3RZ	Duple 340	C57F	1986	
D325ACK	Hestair Duple 425 SDA1510	Duple 425	C53F	1987	
E255MMM	Leyland Tiger TRCL10/3ARZA	Van Hool Alizee H	C50FT	1988	
F814TMD	Volvo B10M-60	Plaxton Paramount 3200 III	C57F	1989	

Previous Registrations:-

LIL2836	B380AMH	**RIB1736**	GBM113T	**RIB1737**	MNM39V	**UHM79**	OLJ193W
LIL4348	A150RMJ					

Named Vehicles:- PRO444W   The Lacey Lady   E255MMM Lacey's Pullman.

Livery:- Grey with red and white relief.

LEASIDE TRAVEL

Leaside Bus Company Ltd, 16 Watsons Road, Wood Green, London, N22 4TZ   *Previous Owner*

DI4	P754RWU	DAF DE33WSSB3000	Ikarus 350	C53F	1997	
DP1	N551LUA	DAF DE33WSSB3000	Plaxton Premiere 350	C49FT	1996	
DP2	N552LUA	DAF DE33WSSB3000	Plaxton Premiere 350	C49FT	1996	
DP3	P753RWU	DAF DE33WSSB3000	Plaxton Premiere 350	C53F	1997	
TPL1	124CLT	Leyland Tiger TRCTL11/3ARZM	Plaxton Paramount 3200 III	C53F	1989	London Buses, 1994
TPL2	361CLT	Leyland Tiger TRCTL11/3ARZM	Plaxton Paramount 3200 III	C53F	1989	London Buses, 1994
TPL8	VLT18	Leyland Tiger TRCL10/3ARZA	Plaxton Paramount 3200 III	C53F	1991	London Buses, 1994
VPL1	C874CYX	Volvo B10M-61	Plaxton Paramount 3200 II	C53F	1986	Grey-Green, 1997
VPL2	C876CYX	Volvo B10M-61	Plaxton Paramount 3200 II	C53F	1986	Grey-Green, 1997

Previous Registrations:- **124CLT** G661WMD   **361CLT** G662WMD   **VLT18** H643GRO

Livery:- Red, white and blue.

LEOLINE TRAVEL

D.A. Baker, Upper Sunbury Road, Hampton, Middlesex, TW12 2DW   *Previous Owner*

341LTL	Volvo B10M-61	Jonckheere Jubilee P50	C51FT	1983	Good News Travels, Hull, 1993
RJI8032	Leyland Royal Tiger	Plaxton Paramount 3500	C49FT	1984	Brewers, 1996
IIB8566	Volvo B10M-61	Caetano Algarve	C49FT	1986	Irvine, Law, 1994
GFE622	Volvo B10M-61	Jonckheere Deauville P599	C51FT	1988	Euroclub, Bilston, 1996
F818OJF	Toyota Coaster HB31R	Caetano Optimo	C20F	1988	Link Line, Harlesden, 1994

Previous Registrations:-

GFE622	F954RNV, NIW8539	**341LTL**	UTN940Y, GNT708, LAG236Y, EOF341	**RJI8032**	A840SYR, FDZ985
IIB8566	C676KDS				

Livery:- White with red fleetnames.

LEWIS OF GREENWICH

Lewis (Greenwich) Ltd, 2-10, Denham Street, Greenwich, London, SE10 0RJ   *Previous Owner*

IIW783	AEC Reliance 6U3ZR	Willowbrook Crusader (1990)	C53F	1973	
IIW6791	AEC Reliance 6U3ZR	Plaxton Supreme III	C53F	1977	RACS, Plumstead, 1983
SPU443W	Ford R1114	Plaxton Supreme IV	C47DL	1980	Freelance Coach Travel, Rochford, 1997
IIW670	Leyland Tiger TRCTL11/3R	Duple Goldliner IV	C55F	1982	Rogers, Martley, 1995
LIW4291	Volvo B10M-61	Duple Goldliner IV	C53F	1982	Abba, Eltham, 1997
PYV277	Leyland Tiger TRCTL11/3RZ	Plaxton Paramount 3500 II	C51DTL	1986	Thames Transit, 1995
IIW372	Volvo B10M-61	Caetano Algarve	C49FT	1986	Renton, Edinburgh, 1996
686CXV	Hestair-Duple 425 SDAK1504	Duple 425	C59F	1986	Cedar, Bedford, 1996
TJL800	DAF MBFL200	Plaxton Paramount 3500 II	C49F	1986	Filer, Ilfracombe, 1996
HIL8286	Volvo B10M-61	Plaxton Paramount 3500 II	C49FT	1986	Filer, Ilfracombe, 1997
IIW628	Leyland Tiger TRCTL11/3RH	Plaxton Paramount 3500 III	C51FT	1987	Thames Transit, 1995
E322OPR	Volvo B10M-61	Duple 320	C53FT	1988	Trent Valley, Rugeley,1997
E418JKS	Volvo B10M-61	Van Hool Alizee H	C49FT	1988	Rennie, Dunfermline, 1997

Previous registrations:-

E418JKS	E743TCS, 439BUS	**IIW628**	D142PTT	**LIW4291**	FHS748X
686CXV	D500NYS	**IIW670**	LCA181Y, 50ABK, UUY142Y	**PYV277**	C128KJD
HIL8286	C122ORM	**IIW783**	UMT903M, IIW670, YYY563N	**TJL800**	C700MVH
IIW372	C660KDS, HIL8442, C995WKS	**IIW6791**	UGP98R		

Livery:- White with blue relief. Upon repaint, coaches now carry 'Lewis of Greenwich - Home of the Millennium' signwriting.

LINK LINE

Link Line Coaches Ltd, 1 Wrottesley Road, Harlesden, London, NW10 5XA   *Previous Owner*

G841VAY	Mercedes-Benz 609D	Reeve Burgess Beaver	C23F	1989	
G474XLF	Mercedes-Benz 609D	Mellor	C19F	1989	Amanda, Bedfont, 1994
VIB7471	Mercedes-Benz 811D	Optare StarRider	C29F	1990	Wings, Uxbridge, 1994
VIB7472	Mercedes-Benz 811D	Optare StarRider	C29F	1990	Wings, Uxbridge, 1994
L4SLT	Toyota Coaster HZB50R	Caetano Optimo III	C16F	1994	Arrowline, Knutsford, 1995
L5SLT	Toyota Coaster HZB50R	Caetano Optimo III	C21F	1994	Arrowline, Knutsford, 1995
R177TKU	Volvo B10M-62	Plaxton Premiere 350	C49FT	1997	
R188TKU	Volvo B10M-62	Plaxton Premiere 350	C49FT	1997	

Previous Registrations:- **VIB7471**   G839LWR, WLT732, G118CLD   **VIB7472**   G383ALM, WLT852, G119CLD

Livery:- White with maroon and gold relief.

LOGANS

Logans Tours Ltd, 1 & 2 The Cottages, Northfleet Green, Southfleet, Kent, DA13 9PT   *Previous Owner*

208MYC	DAF SB2300DHS585	Van Rooijen Odysee	C44FT	1985	London Cityrama, Battersea, 1994
SJI3927	DAF SB2300DHS585	Van Rooijen Odysee	C49FT	1985	Bolton, Southall, 1994
RAZ7243	MCW Metroliner DR140/1	MCW 400 GT	CH54/17DT	1986	West Midlands Travel, 1997

On order is a RABA/Ikarus 350 C48FT which will be the first right hand drive example of this chassis imported into Britain from Hungary.

Previous Registrations:-

RAZ7243   D932ODA   **SJI3927**   B971NPB, JRD1, B971NPB

Livery:- White with multicolour relief.

LONDON COACHES (KENT)

London Coaches (Kent) Ltd, Lower Road, Northfleet, Kent, DA11 9SN   *Previous Owner*

DK1-13	DAF SB220LC550	Ikarus CitiBus	DP42F	1992/4	London Coaches, Wandsworth, 1996

1	J801KHD	4	J804KHD	6	J806KHD	8	J808KHD	10	J810KHD	12	L512KJX	13	L513KJX
3	J803KHD	5	J805KHD	7	J807KHD	9	J809KHD	11	L511KJX				

J432NCP	DAF SB2305DHS585	Van Hool Alizee H	C53F	1992	London Coaches, Wandsworth, 1996
J433NCP	DAF SB2305DHS585	Van Hool Alizee H	C53F	1992	London Coaches, Wandsworth, 1996
J434NCP	DAF SB2305DHS585	Van Hool Alizee H	C53F	1992	London Coaches, Wandsworth, 1996
J435NCP	DAF SB2305DHS585	Van Hool Alizee H	C53F	1992	London Coaches, Wandsworth, 1996
J784KHD	DAF SB3000DKV601	Van Hool Alizee H	C53F	1992	London Coaches, Wandsworth, 1996
J785KHD	DAF SB3000DKV601	Van Hool Alizee H	C53F	1992	London Coaches, Wandsworth, 1996

	DAF SB3000DKV601	Van Hool Alizee HE	C53F	1993	London Coaches, Wandsworth, 1996

K512RJX	K513RJX	K514RJX	K542RJX	K543RJX	K544RJX

	DAF SB3000DKVF601	Van Hool Alizee HE	C55F (L550/552 are C51FT)	1993	London Coaches, Wandsworth, 1996

L548EHD	L549EHD	L550EHD	L551EHD	L552EHD	L553EHD	L554EHD

	DAF SB3000WS601		Van Hool Alizee HE	C55F	1994	London Coaches, Wandsworth, 1996
M571RCP	M573RCP	M575RCP	M577RCP	M578RCP	M579RCP	M580RCP
M572RCP	M574RCP	M576RCP				

	DAF DE33WSSB3000		Van Hool Alizee HE	C55F	1994	London Coaches, Wandsworth, 1996
M736RCP	M738RCP	M739RCP	M740RCP	M741RCP	M745RCP	M746RCP
M737RCP						

	DAF DE33WSSB3000		Ikarus 350	C53F	1996	
N501LUA	N504LUA	N507LUA	P710RWU	P713RWU	P715RWU	P717RWU
N502LUA	N505LUA	N508LUA	P711RWU	P714RWU	P716RWU	P718RWU
N503LUA	N506LUA	N509LUA	P712RWU			

	DAF DE33WSSB3000		Van Hool Alizee HE	C49FT	1996	
P719RWU	P720RWU	P721RWU	P722RWU			

	DAF DE33WSSB3000		Ikarus 350	C53F	1997	
P156RWR	P159RWR	P162RWR	P164RWR	R171GNW	R173GNW	R175GNW
P157RWR	P160RWR	P163RWR	P165RWR	R172GNW	R174GNW	R176GNW
P158RWR	P161RWR					

	DAF DE33WSSB3000		Plaxton Premiere 350	C53F	1997	
P166RWR	P167RWR	P168RWR	P169RWR	P170RWR		

Livery:-   Red with white and black North Kent Express fleetnames

Special Liveries:-

Red with gold London Coaches fleetnames:- K542RJX.
Red with white and gold London Coaches (Kent) fleetnames:- L552EHD, M579/80RCP, P719-22RWU, P156-60RWR, P166-70 RWR.
Red with white and blue Big Value Tours fleetnames:- P164/5RWR
DK class are red, white and grey with Expresslink logos.

THE LONDONERS

						Previous Owner
The Londoners Ltd, 1a Brabourn Grove, Nunhead, London, SE15 2BS
The Londoners Tacho Centre Ltd, 1a Brabourn Grove, Nunhead, London, SE15 2BS

						Previous Owner
H46HKE	MAN 10.180		Berkhof Excellence 1000 Midi	C31FT	1991	The Kings Ferry, Gillingham, 1995
	Volvo B10M-60		Plaxton Premiere 350	C48FT	1992	Wallace Arnold, 1996
J715CWT	J716CWT	J718CWT	J718EUA	J720EUA		

J96UBL	Dennis Javelin 12SDA2101	Berkhof Excellence 2000	C53F	1992	
J97UBL	Dennis Javelin 12SDA2101	Berkhof Excellence 2000	C53F	1992	
J98UBL	Dennis Javelin 12SDA2101	Berkhof Excellence 2000	C53F	1992	
M725LYP	Dennis Javelin 12SDA2131	Plaxton Premiere 320	C53F	1994	
M951SBL	Dennis Javelin 12SDA2134	Berkhof Excellence 1000 LD	C51FT	1995	
M308SHN	Dennis Javelin 12SDA2125	Plaxton Premiere 350	C57F	1995	Walton, Stockton, 1996
M784SRX	Dennis Javelin 12SDA2134	Berkhof Excellence 1000 LD	C51FT	1995	
N9LON	Dennis Javelin 12SDA2155	Berkhof Excellence 1000	C53F	1996	
N10LON	Dennis Javelin 12SDA2134	Berkhof Excellence 1000 LD	C51FT	1996	
N11LON	Dennis Javelin 12SDA2155	Berkhof Excellence 1000	C51FT	1996	
P12LON	Dennis Javelin SFD321BR3TGJ4	Berkhof Axial	C36FT	1997	
P13LON	Dennis Javelin SFD721BR3TGJ3	Berkhof Excellence 1000 L	C57F	1997	
P14LON	Dennis Javelin SFD721BR3TGJ3	Berkhof Excellence 1000 L	C57F	1997	

Previous Registrations:-

H46HKE H8KFC   **J718EUA** J723CWT, 4030WA   **J720EUA** J720CWT, 7820WA   **P12LON** P757HND

Livery:- Dark purple and white with lilac relief. Special Livery:- Kuoni (white)- M308SHN

LONDON PULLMAN

						Previous Owner
London Pullman Tours Ltd, 8 Stanmore Close, Ascot, Berkshire, SL5 9EU

						Previous Owner
H2TCC	Kassbohrer Setra S215HD		Kassbohrer Tornado	C49FT	1991	Travellers, Hounslow, 1996

Previous Registration:- **H2TCC** H809GFW

Livery:- White with orange signwriting.

M & M

M.C. Burcombe, 33 Hitherwell Drive, Harrow Weald, Middlesex, HA3 6JD

P66MNM	Scania K113CRB	Berkhof Axial	C50FT	1996

Livery:- Metallic blue with red fleetname.

M.T.P.

M.T. Powis, 45 Grosvenor Road, Wanstead, London, E11 2EW

Previous Owner

MXI 708	Kassbohrer Setra S215HD	Kassbohrer Tornado	C49FT	1988	GN Coaches, Greenford, 1991
L193NEO	Toyota Coaster HZB50R	Caetano Optimo III	C18F	1994	Holmeswood, Rufford, 1996

Previous Registrations:- **MXI708**   E61JPG

Livery:- Maroon and silver (MXI708) or white (L193NEO).

MASON'S

R.J. Mason, 36 Barmouth Avenue, Perivale, Middlesex, UB6 8JT

Previous Owner

ENC891Y	Ford Transit	Dixon Lomas	M12	1983	
TIB8563	Scania K112CRS	Jonckheere Jubilee P599	C49FT	1984	Scancoaches, North Acton, 1993
C210JVS	Ford Transit	Chassis Developments	M12	1986	
E111VNT	Ford Transit	Whittaker	M12	1987	Elcock, Madeley, 1992
F454NLP	Ford Transit	Ford	M8	1989	private owner, 1993
G57GET	Leyland-DAF 400	Crystals	M16	1989	Browne, Yiewsley, 1995
H742ANX	Talbot Express	Adams	M8	1990	Browne, Yiewsley, 1997
H929BCD	Leyland-DAF 400	Concept	M16	1991	Browne, Yiewsley, 1995
J628PGS	Leyland-DAF 400	Leyland-DAF	M16	1991	Browne, Yiewsley, 1997

Previous Registration:- **TIB8563**   B65MLT

Livery:-   White

MELLOR

S. Mellor, 4 Primrose Close, Harrow, Middlesex, HA2 9AT   *Previous Owner*

| 4233FM | DAF SB3000DKV601 | Jonckheere Deauville P599 | C51FT | 1988 | Buddens, Romsey, 1995 |

Previous Registration:- **4233FM** F956RNV, SJI8118

Livery:- Silver, blue and black.

METROBUS

Metrobus Ltd. Farnborough Hill, Orpington, Kent, BR6 6DA   *Previous Owner*

E575FTW	Ford Transit	Ford	M11	1988	private owner, 1990
E957GGX	DAF MB230DKVL615	Duple 320	C57F	1988	
E597LVH	DAF MB230DKVL615	Duple 320	C57F	1988	KF Cars, Gatwick, 1991
H220JLJ	Leyland Tiger TRCL10/3ARZA	Plaxton 321	C57F	1990	
J201FMX	Leyland Tiger TRCL10/3ARZM	Plaxton 321	C53F	1991	
J202FMX	Leyland Tiger TRCL10/3ARZM	Plaxton 321	C53F	1991	
J51SNY	Leyland Tiger TRCL10/3ARZM	Plaxton 321	C53F	1991	Bebb, Llantwit Fardre, 1993
J52SNY	Leyland Tiger TRCL10/3ARZM	Plaxton 321	C53F	1991	Bebb, Llantwit Fardre, 1993
J577PNK	Ford Transit	Ford	M11	1992	private owner, 1994
K203GMX	Dennis Javelin 12SDA2117	Plaxton Premiere 320	C49FT	1993	
K204GMX	Dennis Javelin 12SDA2117	Plaxton Premiere 320	C49FT	1993	
K205GMX	Dennis Javelin 12SDA2117	Plaxton Premiere 320	C49FT	1993	
K206GMX	Dennis Javelin 12SDA2117	Plaxton Premiere 320	C49FT	1993	
M208BGK	Dennis Javelin 12SDA2131	Plaxton Premiere 320	C53F	1994	
M209BGK	Dennis Javelin 12SDA2131	Plaxton Premiere 320	C53F	1994	
M210BGK	Mercedes-Benz 711D	Plaxton Beaver	C25F	1995	
N211HGO	Dennis Javelin 12SDA2155	Plaxton Premiere 320	C53F	1995	
N212HGO	Dennis Javelin 12SDA2155	Plaxton Premiere 320	C53F	1996	
N213HGO	Dennis Javelin 12SDA2155	Plaxton Premiere 320	C53F	1996	
P214TGP	Dennis Javelin SFD731BR3TGJ2	Plaxton Premiere 350	C49FT	1997	
P215TGP	Dennis Javelin SFD731BR3TGJ2	Plaxton Premiere 350	C49FT	1997	

E575FTW is a crew shuttle bus.

The bus fleet can be found in the *London Bus Handbook*.

Livery:- Blue, white and yellow.   Special liveries:- Hoverspeed City Sprint (White with red and blue relief) :- K204-206 GMX

MITCHAM BELLE

Wimco Group (Coaches) Ltd, 223 Streatham Road, Mitcham, Surrey, CR4 2AJ

Reg	Chassis	Body	Seating	Year	Previous Owner
RHV990R	Leyland Leopard PSU3C/4R	Plaxton Supreme III	C53F	1977	Lewis, Carshalton, 1992
XHT26T	Bedford YMT	Plaxton Supreme IV	C53F	1979	Rokeby School, Coombe, 1996
BGY591T	Leyland Leopard PSU5C/4R	Plaxton Supreme IV	C50F	1979	National Travel London, 1983
KGP305T	Leyland Leopard PSU5C/4R	Plaxton Supreme IV	C55F	1979	Turbostyle, Crawley, 1996
EPM143V	AEC Reliance 6U2R	Plaxton Supreme IV Express	C53F	1979	Hardings, Betchworth, 1991
GPK666V	Bedford YMT	Plaxton Supreme IV	C53F	1980	Wright, Worthing, 1994
B824WYH	Leyland Cub CU335	Wadham Stringer Vanguard	B23FL	1984	Royal Borough of Kensington & Chelsea, 1993
E846PPR	Ford Transit	Ford	M14	1989	Tern Rent-a-Car, Norwich, 1991
F787DNG	Leyland-DAF 400	Crystals	M16	1989	Sanders, Holt, 1996
F605SLP	Ford Transit	Ford	M8	1989	private owner, 1995
JSK957	Dennis Javelin 12SDA1907	Duple 320	C53F	1989	Maybury, Cranborne, 1993
JSK958	Dennis Javelin 12SDA1907	Duple 320	C53F	1989	Maybury, Cranborne, 1993
MIB767	Leyland Tiger TRCL10/3ARZA	Plaxton Paramount 3500 III	C53F	1989	Speedlink, 1997
MIB3534	Leyland Tiger TRCL10/3ARZA	Plaxton Paramount 3500 III	C53F	1989	Speedlink, 1997
F50YEL	Ford Transit	Ford	M14	1989	
F51YEL	Ford Transit	Ford	M14	1989	
F52YEL	Ford Transit	Ford	M14	1989	
F53YEL	Ford Transit	Ford	M14	1989	
G353ARE	Ford Transit	Ford	M11	1990	Javelin, Battersea, 1995
H755FLL	Ford Transit	Ford	M8	1990	London Borough of Merton, 1992
H766VGP	Leyland-DAF 200	Leyland-DAF	M12	1990	private owner, 1995
H642GLE	Ford Transit	Ford	M9	1991	London Borough of Merton, 1993
H128YGG	Ford Transit	Deansgate	M15	1991	private owner, 1995
J28RFD	Leyland-DAF 400	Jubilee (1994)	M16	1991	Field, Cromer, 1994
J781EGP	Iveco TurboDaily 49.12	Frank Guy	C15C	1992	Hotelink, Crawley, 1996
J782EGP	Iveco TurboDaily 49.12	Frank Guy	C15C	1992	Hotelink, Crawley, 1996
J789EGP	Iveco TurboDaily 49.12	Frank Guy	C15C	1992	Hotelink, Crawley, 1996
J790EGP	Iveco TurboDaily 49.12	Frank Guy	C15C	1992	Hotelink, Crawley, 1996
K755SWD	Leyland-DAF 400	Jubilee	M16	1992	
M618DPN	Iveco Daily 40.10	Devon Conversions	M15L	1995	
M619DPN	Iveco Daily 40.10	Devon Conversions	M15L	1995	
M269FNS	Mercedes-Benz 609D	Onyx	C24FL	1995	
M270FNS	Mercedes-Benz 609D	Concept	C24FL	1995	
P158RGN	LDV Convoy	LDV	M16	1996	
P162RGN	LDV Convoy	LDV	M16	1996	
P175NAK	Dennis Javelin	Plaxton Premiere 320	C53F	1997	

Previous Registrations:-

JSK957	F492WPR	**JSK958**	F239OFP	**MIB767**	F635UBL	**MIB3534**	F634UBL	**XHT26T**	DYA978T, 7636LJ

Livery:- White or silver with orange, blue and grey relief.

NAUGHTON'S

Naughton Minicoach Services Ltd, 52 Walsingham Gardens, Stoneleigh, Surrey, KT19 0LU   *Previous Owner*

PDT825X	Ford R1114	Plaxton Supreme V	C53F	1982	Bowers, Chapel-en-le-Frith, 1985
F865ONR	TAZ D3200	TAZ Dubrava	C53F	1989	Heslop, Maida Vale, 1995
F630SAY	Dennis Javelin 11SDL1905	Duple 320	C55F	1989	

Livery:- Various.

NEW BHARAT COACHES

New Bharat Coaches Ltd, 1 Priory Way, Southall, Middlesex, UB2 5HN   *Previous Owner*

D254HFX	Volvo B10M-61	Plaxton Paramount 3200 III	C53F	1987	Essex Coachways, Bow, 1992
E308DMA	Volvo B10M-61	Plaxton Paramount 3500 III	C55F	1988	Vale of Llangollen, 1997
KAZ6914	Volvo B10M-61	Plaxton Paramount 3500 III	C53F	1988	Park, Hamilton, 1993
KAZ6912	Volvo B10M-61	Plaxton Paramount 3500 III	C49FT	1988	Brandon, Blackmore End, 1993
F214NLE	Volvo B10M-61	Plaxton Paramount 3500 III	C53F	1988	
KAZ6911	Volvo B10M-61	Plaxton Paramount 3500 III	C53F	1989	Travellers, Hounslow, 1993
KAZ6913	Volvo B10M-60	Plaxton Paramount 3500 III	C49FT	1989	Atkinson, Ingleby Arncliffe, 1995
F442DUG	Volvo B10M-60	Plaxton Paramount 3500 III	C51FT	1989	Porteous, Anlaby, 1996
N21EYB	Volvo B10M-62	Van Hool Alizee HE	C49FT	1996	

Previous Registrations:-

| **E308DMA** | E420CCA, VLT250 | **KAZ6912** | F661LAR | **KAX6913** | F39LCA | **KAZ6914** | E597UHS |
| **KAZ6911** | F104CCL | | | | | | |

Livery:-   Cream and yellow.   Special Livery:- N21EYB   Silver with multicolour flashes.

NOSTALGIABUS

Nostalgiabus Ltd, 228 Cannon Hill Lane, Merton Park, London, SW20 9BY   *Previous Owner*

	KYE905	Bedford OB	Duple Vista	C27F	1949	preservation, 1997
RF136	MLL523	AEC Regal IV 9821LT	Metro-Cammell	B39F	1952	preservation, 1991
7	MXX367	Guy Special NLLVP	Eastern Coach Works	B26F	1954	preservation, 1991
	YVS288	AEC Routemaster R2RH	Park Royal	H36/28R	1960	Watford & District, 1997
	WFO410	AEC Routemaster R2RH	Park Royal	H36/24R	1961	Watford & District, 1997
RM1183	183CLT	AEC Routemaster R2RH	Park Royal	H36/28R	1962	London & Country, 1996
RMC1462	462CLT	AEC Routemaster R2RH	Park Royal	H32/35RD	1962	preservation, 1991

	394CLT	AEC Routemaster R2RH	Park Royal	H36/24R	1963	Watford & District, 1997
	571CLT	AEC Routemaster R2RH	Park Royal	H36/24R	1963	Watford & District, 1997
	CUV156C	AEC Routemaster R2RH	Park Royal	H36/24R	1965	Watford & District, 1997
	CUV180C	AEC Routemaster R2RH	Park Royal	H36/24R	1965	Watford & District, 1997
	RHC51S	AEC Reliance 6U2R	Plaxton Supreme III	C53F	1977	Thomas, West Ewell, 1992
	THX333s	Leyland Fleetline FE30ALR	MCW	H44/24D	1978	Hodge, South Mimms, 1996
LW92	B102SED	Leyland Olympian ONLXB/2R	East Lancashire	DPH47/31F	1985	Warrington, 1996

Previous Registrations:- **WFO410**   WLT378   **YVS288**   WLT357, EDS278A

Livery:- Various.

ON TIME

On Time Ltd, 156/8 Wandsworth Bridge Road, Wandsworth, London, SW6 2UH

C72SPK	Volkswagen Caravelle	Volkswagen	M8	1991	
M361LPC	Mercedes-Benz 711D	Olympus	C24F	1995	
P743LKL	Mercedes-Benz 814D	Robin Hood RH2000	C25F	1997	
P894PWW	DAF DE33WSSB3000	Van Hool Alizee HE	C51FT	1997	
P897PWW	EOS E180Z	EOS 90	C51FT	1997	
P218RWR	EOS E180Z	EOS 90	C49FT	1997	
P840SUC	Volkswagen Kombi	Advanced Vehicle Builders	M11	1997	
P870SUC	Volkswagen Kombi	Advanced Vehicle Builders	M11	1997	

Livery:- White with green fleetnames.

P & R

P.& R. Coaches, 20 Abbotts Road, Mitcham, Surrey, CR4 1JP   *Previous Owner*

RXI4615	Volvo B58-61	Plaxton Supreme IV	C57F	1980	Kent Coach Tours, Ashford, 1996
LBK145Y	Mercedes-Benz L608D	Robin Hood	C19F	1982	Coach Companions, Worcester Park, 1997
5398TW	Volvo B10M-61	Jonckheere Jubilee P90	CH48/9FT	1983	Wilson, Middlesbrough, 1991
IIL4589	DAF MB230DKFL615	Duple 340	C53FT	1986	Drayton Vale, Ratby, 1996
L538XBX	Leyland-DAF 400	Cymric	M16	1994	private owner, 1996

Previous Registrations:- **IIL4589**   D617SJX   **RXI4615**   HTV15V   **5398TW**   NNV602Y

Livery:- Green and white.

PANORAMA

G.R. Harris, 285 Aldborough Road South, Seven Kings, Essex, IG3 8JD

F498RML	Volvo B10M-60	Plaxton Paramount 3200 III	C53F	1989	
H828RWJ	Scania K93CRB	Plaxton Paramount 3200 III	C53F	1991	
M328VET	Scania K93CRB	Van Hool Alizee HE	C53F	1995	

Livery:- Light blue and grey.

PEACOCK

C.S. & F.S. Peacock, 85 Totterdown Street, Tooting, London, SW17 8TB   *Previous Owner*

DGD99T	Volvo B58-61	Plaxton Supreme IV	C50FT	1979	Hollingshead, Aintree, 1995
YJB121	Volvo B10M-61	Plaxton Supreme IV	C53F	1982	Wootton, Northampton, 1996

Previous Registration:- **YJB121** NBL903X

Livery:- White with two tone blue relief.

PEMICO TRAVEL (including Peckham Mini Coaches)

R.G. Sault & Mrs. P.R. Roff, 9-11 Verney Road, Bermondsey, London, SE16 3DH   *Previous Owner*

FIL4138	Bedford YMP	Plaxton Paramount 3200 II	C28F	1985	Armchair, Brentford, 1990
FIL4139	Bedford YMP	Plaxton Paramount 3200 II	C28F	1985	Armchair, Brentford, 1990
E249NUU	Mercedes-Benz 307D	Made To Measure	M12	1987	
E250NUU	Mercedes-Benz 307D	Made To Measure	M12	1987	
E509NUW	Mercedes-Benz 307D	Made To Measure	M12	1987	
NIL4809	Mercedes-Benz 408D	Devon Conversions	C16F	1990	Inter-European Airways, Cardiff, 1994
J553HGX	Ford Transit	Ford	M12	1992	
L206LOX	Leyland-DAF 400	Leyland-DAF	M16	1994	Churchfields Rentals, 1996
L146OUM	Mercedes-Benz 609D	Autobus Classique	C23F	1994	

	LDV 400		LDV		M16	1994		
L426VWV	L427VWV	L428VWV	L429VWV	L430VWV	L431VWV	L432VWV		

	LDV 400		LDV		M16	1994	
M416BCD	M417BCD	M418BCD	M419BCD	M420BCD			

M351TDO	Mercedes-Benz 814D	Autobus Classique II	C33F	1994
M352TDO	Mercedes-Benz 814D	Autobus Classique II	C33F	1994

	Dennis Javelin SFD731BR3VGJ9	Plaxton Excalibur	C49FT	1997
P989NKU	P991NKU	P993NKU	P995NKU	P996NKU	P997NKU	P998NKU
P990NKU	P992NKU	P994NKU				

On Order:- Mercedes-Benz Vario 0.814D/Crystals C16FT.

Previous Registrations:-

FIL4138	B409CMC	NIL4809	G508JHB		E250NUU	E971SVU, LIL4233	E509NUW	E972SVU, LIL4235
FIL4139	B410CMC	E249NUU	E973SVU, LIL4234			

Livery:- White.

PHOENIX

S.S. Wassef, 48 Rathmell Drive, Clarence Avenue, Clapham, London, SW4 8JN   *Previous Owner*

PRO446W	Bedford YLQ	Duple Dominant II	C35F	1980	Andes, Camberwell, 1996
VIB3294	Bova EL28/581	Duple Calypso	C53F	1984	McVay, Edinburgh, 1994
NIW5691	DAF SB3000DKSB585	LAG Panoramic	C49FT	1986	Blueways, Battersea, 1996
K324NKB	Mercedes-Benz 709D	North West Coach Sales	C21F	1992	Roberts, Bootle, 1996

Previous Registrations:- **NIW5691**   C749VDO   **VIB3294**   8874PH, A37HPL, LIB9415

Named Vehicle:- NIW5691   Sue

Livery:- Pink and white with blue relief.

PRAIRIE

Prairie Coaches Ltd, Unit 3, Green Lane, Hounslow, Middlesex, TW4 6BY

					Previous Owner
EAC876T	Bedford YMT	Plaxton Supreme IV Express	C53F	1979	Shoestock, Ickenham, 1990
FKX285T	Bedford YMT	Duple Dominant II	C53F	1979	
848KMX	Volvo B10M-61	Jonckheere Jubilee P50	C48DT	1983	Travellers, Hounslow, 1991
315ASV	Volvo B10M-61	Jonckheere Jubilee P50	C48DT	1983	Travellers, Hounslow, 1991
PIJ411	Volvo B10M-61	Van Hool Alizee H	C49FT	1984	Moon, Horsham, 1992
SIJ701	Volvo B9M	Plaxton Paramount 3200 II	C43F	1985	Capital, West Drayton, 1991
FIL7665	Bova FHD12-280	Bova Futura	C49FT	1986	Collier, Earith, 1993
PJI1824	Volvo B10M-61	Plaxton Paramount 3200 III	C53F	1987	New Bharat, Southall, 1997
E178WDV	Leyland Tiger TRCTL11/3RZ	Duple 320	C54FT	1987	Turner, Chumleigh, 1997
CCC257	Volvo B10M-61	Ikarus Blue Danube 336	C49FT	1989	Sutherland, Edinburgh, 1994
SRP209	Volvo B10M-61	Ikarus Blue Danube 336	C53F	1989	Sutherland, Edinburgh, 1994
H201DVM	Van Hool T815	Van Hool Alicron	C53F	1989	Shearings, 1995
H202DVM	Van Hool T815	Van Hool Alicron	C53F	1991	Shearings, 1995
J53NJT	Volvo B10M-60	Plaxton Excalibur	C49FT	1992	Jones, Market Drayton, 1997

Previous Registrations:

315ASV	ONV643Y	**J53NJT**	A3XEL	**PJI411**	A186MNE	**SRP209**	F110SSE
CCC257	F109SSE	**848KMX**	ONV641Y	**SIJ701**	C160TLF	**PJI1824**	D570MVR, ESU117, D464GEN
FIL7665	C972TPV						

Livery:- White and turquoise with yellow signwriting.

PREMIER-ALBANIAN

Premier Coaches (Watford) Ltd, 105-107 Queens Avenue, Watford, Hertfordshire, WD1 7NU

					Previous Owner
ENT778	Leyland Tiger PS1	Burlingham	C33F	1948	Combs, Ixworth, 1972
LTA904	Bedford OB	Duple Vista	C27F	1949	Rover, Chesham, 1988
LGV994	Bedford SB3	Duple Vega	C41F	1958	Wents, Boxted, 1982
CBM12X	Leyland Tiger TRCTL11/3R	Plaxton Supreme VI	C53F	1982	
CBM13X	Leyland Tiger TRCTL11/3R	Plaxton Supreme VI	C53F	1982	
B21XKX	Leyland Tiger TRCTL11/3R	Plaxton Paramount 3200	C57F	1985	
B22XKX	Leyland Tiger TRCTL11/3R	Plaxton Paramount 3200	C57F	1985	
C24GKX	Iveco 79.14	Caetano Viana	C19F	1986	

Livery:- Red and cream.

Q DRIVE COACHES

Q Drive Coaches Ltd, Waterford House, Erftstadt Court, Wokingham, Berkshire, RG11 2XJ   *Previous Owner*

Limebourne fleet:-

G976LRP	Volvo B10M-60	Jonckheere Deauville P599	C53F	1990	Scancoaches, North Acton, 1997
G977LRP	Volvo B10M-60	Jonckheere Deauville P599	C53F	1990	Scancoaches, North Acton, 1997
G978LRP	Volvo B10M-60	Jonckheere Deauville P599	C53F	1990	Scancoaches, North Acton, 1997
G826YJF	Bova FHD12-290	Bova Futura	C49FT	1990	London Cityrama, Battersea, 1993
G827YJF	Bova FHD12-290	Bova Futura	C49FT	1990	London Cityrama, Battersea, 1993
K513KWT	Volvo B10M-62	Van Hool Alizee HE	C48FT	1993	Wallace Arnold, 1997
K514KWT	Volvo B10M-62	Van Hool Alizee HE	C48FT	1993	Wallace Arnold, 1997
K807HUM	Volvo B10M-60	Van Hool Alizee HE	C48FT	1993	Wallace Arnold, 1997
K808HUM	Volvo B10M-60	Van Hool Alizee HE	C48FT	1993	Wallace Arnold, 1997
K809HUM	Volvo B10M-60	Van Hool Alizee HE	C48FT	1993	Wallace Arnold, 1996
K810HUM	Volvo B10M-60	Van Hool Alizee HE	C48FT	1993	Wallace Arnold, 1996
K811HUM	Volvo B10M-60	Van Hool Alizee HE	C48FT	1993	Wallace Arnold, 1996
K817HUM	Volvo B10M-60	Van Hool Alizee HE	C48FT	1993	Wallace Arnold, 1996
K819HUM	Volvo B10M-60	Van Hool Alizee HE	C48FT	1993	Wallace Arnold, 1996
K820HUM	Volvo B10M-60	Van Hool Alizee HE	C48FT	1993	Wallace Arnold, 1996
L982OGY	Bova FLD12-270	Bova Futura	C53F	1994	
L987OGY	Bova FHD12-340	Bova Futura	C53F	1994	
L992OGY	Bova FLD12-270	Bova Futura	C53F	1994	
L993OGY	Bova FLD12-270	Bova Futura	C53F	1994	
L182PMX	Bova FHD12-340	Bova Futura	C53F	1994	
L76RAK	Bova FHD12-340	Bova Futura	C51FT	1994	
L182PMX	Bova FHD12-340	Bova Futura	C53F	1994	
L206RAK	Bova FHD12-340	Bova Futura	C51FT	1994	
M259BGK	Bova FLD12-270	Bova Futura	C53F	1994	
N854XMO	Dennis Javelin 12SDA2161	Berkhof Excellence 1000	C51F	1996	
N855XMO	Dennis Javelin 12SDA2159	Berkhof Excellence 1000	C51F	1996	
N856XMO	Dennis Javelin 12SDA2159	Berkhof Excellence 1000	C51F	1996	
N857XMO	Dennis Javelin 12SDA2159	Berkhof Excellence 1000	C51F	1996	
N858XMO	Dennis Javelin 12SDA2159	Berkhof Excellence 1000	C51F	1996	
N859XMO	Dennis Javelin 12SDA2159	Berkhof Excellence 1000	C51F	1996	
N860XMO	Dennis Javelin 12SDA2159	Berkhof Excellence 1000	C51F	1996	
N861XMO	Dennis Javelin 12SDA2159	Berkhof Excellence 1000	C51F	1996	
N862XMO	Dennis Javelin 12SDA2159	Berkhof Excellence 1000	C51F	1996	
N863XMO	Dennis Javelin 12SDA2159	Berkhof Excellence 1000	C51F	1996	
N864XMO	Dennis Javelin 12SDA2159	Berkhof Excellence 1000	C51F	1996	
N865XMO	Dennis Javelin 12SDA2159	Berkhof Excellence 1000	C51F	1996	
N866XMO	Dennis Javelin 12SDA2159	Berkhof Excellence 1000	C51F	1996	

N867XMO	Dennis Javelin 12SDA2159	Berkhof Excellence 1000	C51F	1996
N868XMO	Dennis Javelin 12SDA2159	Berkhof Excellence 1000	C49F	1996
N869XMO	Dennis Javelin 12SDA2159	Berkhof Excellence 1000	C51F	1996
N870XMO	Dennis Javelin 12SDA2159	Berkhof Excellence 1000	C53F	1996
N871XMO	Dennis Javelin 12SDA2159	Berkhof Excellence 1000	C49F	1996
N872XMO	Dennis Javelin 12SDA2159	Berkhof Excellence 1000	C49F	1996
N873XMO	Dennis Javelin 12SDA2159	Berkhof Excellence 1000	C53F	1996
P875FMO	Volvo B10M-62	Berkhof Axial	C27FT	1997
P876FMO	Volvo B10M-62	Berkhof Axial	C27FT	1997
P877FMO	Volvo B10M-62	Berkhof Axial	C27FT	1997
P878FMO	Volvo B10M-62	Berkhof Axial	C27FT	1997
P879FMO	Volvo B10M-62	Berkhof Axial	C27FT	1997
P881FMO	Dennis Javelin SFD721BR3TGJ2	Berkhof Axial	C51F	1997
P882FMO	Dennis Javelin SFD731BR3TGJ4	Berkhof Axial	C51F	1997
P883FMO	Dennis Javelin SFD731BR3TGJ4	Berkhof Axial	C51F	1997
P884FMO	Dennis Javelin SFD731BR3TGJ4	Berkhof Axial	C51F	1997
P885FMO	Dennis Javelin SFD731BR3TGJ4	Berkhof Axial	C51F	1997
P886FMO	Dennis Javelin SFD731BR3TGJ4	Berkhof Axial	C51F	1997
P887FMO	Dennis Javelin SFD731BR3TGJ4	Berkhof Axial	C51F	1997
P889FMO	Dennis Javelin SFD731BR3TGJ4	Berkhof Axial	C51F	1997
P890FMO	Dennis Javelin SFD731BR3TGJ4	Berkhof Axial	C51F	1997
P891FMO	Dennis Javelin SFD731BR3TGJ4	Berkhof Axial	C51F	1997
P892FMO	Dennis Javelin SFD731BR3TGJ4	Berkhof Axial	C51F	1997
P893FMO	Dennis Javelin SFD731BR3TGJ4	Berkhof Axial	C51F	1997
P894FMO	Dennis Javelin SFD731BR3TGJ4	Berkhof Axial	C51F	1997
P895FMO	Dennis Javelin SFD731BR3TGJ4	Berkhof Axial	C51F	1997
P896FMO	Dennis Javelin SFD731BR3TGJ4	Berkhof Axial	C51F	1997
P897FMO	Dennis Javelin SFD731BR3TGJ4	Berkhof Axial	C51F	1997
P898FMO	Dennis Javelin SFD731BR3TGJ4	Berkhof Axial	C51F	1997
P899FMO	Dennis Javelin SFD731BR3TGJ4	Berkhof Axial	C51F	1997
P901FMO	Dennis Javelin SFD731BR3TGJ4	Berkhof Axial	C51F	1997
P902FMO	Dennis Javelin SFD731BR3TGJ4	Berkhof Axial	C51F	1997
P903FMO	Dennis Javelin SFD731BR3TGJ4	Berkhof Axial	C49F	1997
P904FMO	Dennis Javelin SFD731BR3TGJ4	Berkhof Axial	C49F	1997
P905FMO	Dennis Javelin SFD731BR3TGJ4	Berkhof Axial	C49F	1997
P906FMO	Dennis Javelin SFD731BR3TGJ4	Berkhof Axial	C51F	1997
P347KCF	Dennis Javelin SFD731BR3TGJ4	Berkhof Axial	C51FT	1997

The Limebourne bus fleet can be found in the *London Bus Handbook*

Scan Coach Company fleet

TIB8573	Scania K113CRB	Jonckheere Deauville P599	C24FT	1989	
TIB8574	Scania K113CRB	Jonckheere Deauville P599	C24FT	1989	
TIB8575	Volvo B10M-60	Jonckheere Deauville P599	C32FT	1990	
TIB8576	Volvo B10M-60	Jonckheere Deauville P599	C32FT	1990	
H61XBD	Volvo B10M-60	Jonckheere Deauville P599	C51FT	1991	
H62XBD	Volvo B10M-60	Jonckheere Deauville P599	C51FT	1991	
J78VTX	Kassbohrer Setra S215HD	Kassbohrer Tornado	C49FT	1992	Travellers, Hounslow, 1994
K592VBC	MAN 11.190	Caetano Algarve II	C35F	1993	Limebourne, Battersea, 1997
K593VBC	MAN 11.190	Caetano Algarve II	C35F	1993	Limebourne, Battersea, 1997
L780GMJ	Dennis Javelin 12SDA2117	Plaxton Premiere 320	C57F	1993	Limebourne, Battersea, 1997
L528XUT	Volvo B10M-60	Jonckheere Deauville P599	C51FT	1993	
L529XUT	Volvo B10M-60	Jonckheere Deauville P599	C35FT	1993	
L530XUT	Volvo B10M-60	Jonckheere Deauville P599	C51FT	1993	
CAZ2043	Kassbohrer Setra S210H	Kassbohrer Optimal	C35F	1994	
CAZ2044	Kassbohrer Setra S210H	Kassbohrer Optimal	C35F	1994	
CAZ2045	Kassbohrer Setra S210H	Kassbohrer Optimal	C35F	1994	
CAZ2046	Kassbohrer Setra S210H	Kassbohrer Optimal	C35F	1994	
CAZ2047	Kassbohrer Setra S210H	Kassbohrer Optimal	C35F	1994	
L668PWT	Mercedes-Benz 814D	Optare StarRider	C29F	1994	
L669PWT	Mercedes-Benz 814D	Optare StarRider	C29F	1994	
M151KJF	Toyota Coaster HZB50R	Caetano Optimo III	C18F	1995	
M152KJF	Toyota Coaster HZB50R	Caetano Optimo III	C18F	1995	
M153KJF	Toyota Coaster HZB50R	Caetano Optimo III	C18F	1995	
M154KJF	Toyota Coaster HZB50R	Caetano Optimo III	C18F	1995	
M971NFU	Kassbohrer Setra S250	Kassbohrer Special	C57F	1995	
M972NFU	Kassbohrer Setra S250	Kassbohrer Special	C53F	1995	
M973NFU	Kassbohrer Setra S250	Kassbohrer Special	C57F	1995	
M974NFU	Kassbohrer Setra S250	Kassbohrer Special	C53F	1995	
M975NFU	Kassbohrer Setra S250	Kassbohrer Special	C57F	1995	
M976NFU	Kassbohrer Setra S250	Kassbohrer Special	C48FT	1995	
N874XMO	Dennis Javelin 12SDA2159	Berkhof Excellence 1000LD	C27FT	1996	Limebourne, Battersea, 1997
P875FMO	Volvo B10M-62	Berkhof Axial	C27FT	1997	
P876FMO	Volvo B10M-62	Berkhof Axial	C27FT	1997	
P877FMO	Volvo B10M-62	Berkhof Axial	C27FT	1997	
P878FMO	Volvo B10M-62	Berkhof Axial	C27FT	1997	
P878FMO	Volvo B10M-62	Berkhof Axial	C27FT	1997	
P575GCF	Dennis Javelin 12SDA2136	Berkhof Excellence 1000L	C57F	1997	
P576GCF	Dennis Javelin 12SDA2136	Berkhof Excellence 1000L	C57F	1997	
P633KTF	Volvo B10M-62	Berkhof Axial	C51FT	1997	
P634KTF	Volvo B10M-62	Berkhof Axial	C51FT	1997	

Previous Registrations:-

K513KWT K805HUM, 8665WA
K514KWT K806HUM, 8980WA
TIB8573 F943RNV
TIB8574 F944RNV
TIB8575 G979LRP
TIB8576 G980LRP

Liveries:-   Limebourne:- Metallic dark green with lime green skirt..
              Scan Coach Company:- White with blue relief and grey skirt. (Note. All former Scancoaches vehicles will soon receive the new livery).

Special Liveries:-

Eurobus (White with blue signwriting):- K811/20HUM, L182PMX.
Eurobus (Cream with blue signwriting):- K807-9HUM, K817/9HUM.
Eurobus (Metallic green with lime green relief and white signwriting):- K811HUM, K514KWT
The Glider:- (Red with beige skirt):- N874XMO, P875-9FMO.
Insight (white with blue and yellow signwriting):- N868XMO, N869XMO, N871XMO, N872XMO, P903FMO, P905FMO.
Trafalgar Tours (White with rainbow stripes):- L76RAK, L206RAK, N855-6XMO, N858-60XMO, N863XMO, N865-7XMO, P882-87FMO, P889-91FMO,
                                                P893-8FMO, P347KCF.
White:- L982/7/92/3OGY, M259BGK, N854XMO, N857XMO, N861/2/4/70/3XMO, P881FMO, P892/9FMO, P901/2/4/6FMO.

QUALITY COACHES OF WINDSOR

N. Harris, 5 Bourne Avenue, Windsor, Berkshire, SL4 3JP   *Previous Owner*

| TJI3130 | Van Hool T815 | Van Hool Alizee | C49FT | 1990 | Osborne, Tollesbury, 1996 |

Previous Registrations:-

TJI3130   G430VML

Livery:- White and orange.

RALPHS COACHES

Ralph's Coaches Ltd, Middle Green Trading Estate, Middle Green, Langley, Slough, Berkshire, SL3 6BX   *Previous Owner*

Reg	Chassis	Body	Seating	Year	Previous Owner
WSV468	Volvo B10M-60	Plaxton Paramount 3500 III	C53F	1990	
LAZ6728	Toyota Coaster HDB30R	Caetano Optimo II	C18F	1991	
K815EET	Volvo B10M-60	Van Hool Alizee HE	C48FT	1992	
WSV479	Volvo B10M-46	Van Hool Alizee HE	C36FT	1992	
K936GWR	Mercedes-Benz 814D	Optare StarRider	C28F	1992	
K937GWR	Mercedes-Benz 814D	Optare StarRider	C28F	1992	
K938GWR	Mercedes-Benz 814D	Optare StarRider	C28F	1992	
LIL5930	Mercedes-Benz 814D	Optare StarRider	C28F	1992	
K57BAX	Volvo B10M-60	Plaxton Excalibur	C47FT	1993	Shearings, 1996
K58BAX	Volvo B10M-60	Plaxton Excalibur	C47FT	1993	Shearings, 1996
K61BAX	Volvo B10M-60	Jonckheere Deauville P599	C48FT	1993	Bebb, Llantwit Fardre, 1996
K63BAX	Volvo B10M-60	Jonckheere Deauville P599	C48FT	1993	Bebb, Llantwit Fardre, 1996
L990CRY	Toyota Coaster HZB50R	Caetano Optimo III	C18F	1994	
L991CRY	Toyota Coaster HZB50R	Caetano Optimo III	C18F	1994	
L992CRY	Toyota Coaster HZB50R	Caetano Optimo III	C18F	1994	
L945NWW	Volvo B10M-60	Jonckheere Deauville 45	C50F	1994	Wallace Arnold, 1997
L702SUA	Volvo B12T	Jonckheere Deauville 65	C50FT	1994	Wallace Arnold, 1997
M231UKU	Volvo B10M-62	Plaxton Premiere 350	C48FT	1994	
N749CYA	Volvo B10M-62	Van Hool Alizee HE	C48FT	1995	
N750CYA	Volvo B10M-62	Van Hool Alizee HE	C48FT	1995	
N901NNR	Volvo B6LE	Wright Crusader	DP33F	1995	
N902NNR	Volvo B6LE	Wright Crusader	DP33F	1995	
P773BJF	Toyota Coaster HZB50R	Caetano Optimo III	C18F	1996	
P616FTV	Volvo B10M-62	Plaxton Premiere 350	C53F	1997	
P617FTV	Volvo B10M-62	Plaxton Premiere 350	C53F	1997	
P618FTV	Volvo B10M-62	Plaxton Premiere 350	C53F	1997	
P619FTV	Volvo B10M-62	Plaxton Premiere 350	C48FT	1997	
R960RCH	Volvo B10M-48	Plaxton Premiere 320	C36F	1997	

Previous Registrations:-

LAZ6728 H394CFT   **LIL5930** K939GWR   **WSV468** H161DJU   **WSV479** K816EET   **L702SUA** L965NWW, 4WA

Livery:- White and two tone blue.

Special Liveries:-

Creative Tours (Dark blue):- WSV468
Holiday Inn Heathrow (Maroon and grey) :- N901/2NNR.
Marriott Hotel, Slough (Magenta) :- K935-939GWR.

REDWING COACHES

Pullmanor Ltd, 145-147 Coldharbour Lane, London, SE5 9PD

						Previous Owner	
K401STL	Kassbohrer Setra S210H		Kassbohrer Optimal	C35F	1993	Spirit of London, Hounslow, 1994	
	Volvo B10M-62		Jonckheere Deauville 45	C53F	1994	Park, Hamilton, 1995	
L750YGE	L753YGE	L755YGE	L757YGE	L758YGE			
	Volvo B10M-62		Plaxton Premiere 350	C49FT	1995		
M230LYT	M231LYT	M232LYT	M233LYT	M234LYT	M235LYT		
	Volvo B10M-62		Plaxton Premiere 350	C53F	1996		
N281OYE	N283OYE	N285OYE	N287OYE	N289OYE	N291OYE	N293OYE	
N282OYE	N284OYE	N286OYE	N288OYE	N290OYE	N292OYE	N294OYE	
	Kassbohrer Setra S250		Kassbohrer Special	C53F	1996		
N202PUL	N203PUL	N204PUL	N205PUL	N206PUL	N207PUL		
P208RUU	Mercedes-Benz Vario 0.814D		Autobus Classique Nouvelle	C25F	1997		
	Kassbohrer Setra S250		Kassbohrer Special	C48FT	1997		
P211RUU	P212RUU	P213RUU	P214RUU	P215RUU	P216RUU	P217RUU	

Previous Registrations:-

N288OYE N290OYE
N289OYE N288OYE
N290OYE N289OYE

Livery:- Red and cream.

Special Livery:- Evan Evans Tours (Red and cream):- N281-290OYE

RELIANCE OF GRAVESEND

Reliance Coaches of Gravesend, 45 Darnley Road, Gravesend, Kent, DA11 0SD   *Previous Owner*

GBZ8304	Volvo B10M-61	LAG Galaxy	C49FT	1984	Daish, Shanklin, 1995
PJI3532	Volvo B10M-61	Plaxton Paramount 3200 III	C53F	1988	
IAZ8156	Volvo B10M-60	Plaxton Paramount 3500 III	C53F	1989	Greater Manchester South, 1996
IAZ8157	Volvo B10M-60	Plaxton Paramount 3500 III	C53F	1989	Truronian, Truro, 1996
PJI8635	Volvo B10M-61	Plaxton Paramount 3500 III	C49FT	1989	Ambassador Travel, 1993
TJI5373	Volvo B10M-60	Plaxton Paramount 3200 III	C53F	1989	Frames Rickards, Bloomsbury, 1995
TJI5374	Volvo B10M-60	Plaxton Paramount 3200 III	C53F	1989	Frames Rickards, Bloomsbury, 1995
TJI5375	Volvo B10M-60	Plaxton Paramount 3200 III	C53F	1989	Frames Rickards, Bloomsbury, 1995
L54CNY	Volvo B10M-60	Plaxton Premiere 320	C49FT	1993	Bebb, Llantwit Fardre, 1997

Previous Registrations:-

GBZ8304	A990JJU	**IAZ8157**	NXI9008, F254BHF	**PJI8635**	F103CCL	**TJI5374**	F892SMU
IAZ8156	NXI9003, F256BHF	**PJI3532**	E291OMG	**TJI5373**	F890SMU	**TJI5375**	F893SMU

Livery:- Dark blue and yellow.

REPTON'S COACHES

A.J & E.R.A. Repton, 152 Selbourne Avenue, New Haw, Weybridge, Surrey, KT15 2RT   *Previous Owner*

C699FFJ	Ford Transit	Carlyle	B16F	1986	Devon General, 1996
546FJB	Volvo B10M-61	Van Hool Alizee H	C53F	1986	Blythin, Llandudno Junction, 1997
E604CDS	Volvo B10M-61	Plaxton Paramount 3500 III	C53F	1987	Irvine, Law, 1993
P4REP	Dennis Javelin SFD721BR3TGJ2	Plaxton Premiere 320	C53F	1997	

Named Vehicles:-   C669FFJ   Little Mitch   E604CDS   Lady Ann

Previous Registrations:-   **546FJB**   C533DND   **E604CDS**   E773MMH, 123TRL

Livery: Cream and blue.

REYNOLDS DIPLOMAT

R. Reynolds & S.K. Goodhand, 22 Bushey Hall Road, Bushey, Hertfordshire, WD2 2ED   *Previous Owner*

KIJ56	Leyland Tiger TRCTL11/3R	Plaxton Paramount 3500	C50FT	1983	Vanguard, Bedworth, 1993
B515OEH	Leyland Tiger TRCTL11/3RH	Duple Laser 2	C51F	1984	Hillier, Foxham, 1995
NSU990	Scania K112CRS	Jonckheere Jubilee P599	C53F	1984	Cordery, Heathfield, 1996
NSU991	Scania K112CRS	Jonckheere Jubilee P599	C53F	1984	Cordery, Heathfield, 1996
B839NKA	Leyland Tiger TRCTL11/3RH	Plaxton Paramount 3500 II	C49FT	1985	Blue Triangle, Bootle, 1993
C460CNG	Leyland Tiger TRCTL11/3RZ	Plaxton Paramount 3500 II	C49FT	1986	Rosemary, Terrington St Clements, 1993
NIW4405	Volvo B10M-61	Jonckheere Jubilee P50	C51FT	1986	Thamesdown, 1997
D654SRM	Volvo B10M-61	Plaxton Paramount 3500 II	C55F	1986	Messenger, Aspatria, 1994
A1NYJ	Volvo B10M-60	Duple 340	C53F	1989	Westbus, Hounslow, 1996
J91JFR	Dennis Javelin 12SDA1929	Plaxton Paramount 3200 III LS	C57F	1991	Grimshaw, Burnley, 1994
L3RDC	Mercedes-Benz 814D	Autobus Classique	C33F	1994	
N4RDC	Dennis Javelin 12SDA2136	Berkhof Excellence 1000L	C57F	1995	
N5RDC	Volvo B10M-62	Jonckheere Deauville 45	C51FT	1995	
N6RDC	Scania K113CRB	Irizar Century 12.35	C49FT	1996	

Previous Registrations:-

KIJ56	WWA301Y	**NSU991**	B492CBD	**A1NYJ**	F994UME
NSU990	B491CBD	**NIW4405**	C413LRP	**B839NKA**	B27OBF, 4327PL, B457SFA, 449CLT

Livery:- Green and white with gold relief.

Special Livery:- A1NYJ carries a special livery for the National Youth Jazz Orchestra.

COLIN RICH/SOUTH LONDON COACHES

C.T. Rich, 61 Sandy Lane South, Wallington, Surrey, SM6 9RF   *Previous Owner*

NIB6829	Volvo B10M-61	Duple Goldliner IV	C50FT	1982	T.H.Jones, Pwllheli, 1989
RIB6193	Volvo B10M-61	Jonckheere Jubilee P599	C49FT	1984	Fargo, Rayne, 1992
JIL6819	Leyland Tiger TRCTL11/3R	Duple Caribbean II	C53F	1985	Powner, Hinckley, 1994
LIL7818	Volvo B10M-61	Jonckheere Jubilee P599	C49FT	1987	Westway, Belmont, 1996

Previous Registrations:

JIL6819	B209AFV	**LIL7818**	D30RKX, D29RKX	**NIB6829**	WVT886X	**RIB6193**	A338YDT

Livery:- White with yellow, orange and red releif.

SSS

APA Travel Services Ltd, 138 Eversholt Street, Euston, London, NW1 1BL

Previous Owner

E491GPK	Kassbohrer Setra S215HD	Kassbohrer Tornado	C49FT	1988	Fortmere, Uxbridge, 1991
F179OVL	Kassbohrer Setra S215HR	Kassbohrer Rational	C53F	1989	
H878GTM	Mercedes-Benz 0303/15	Plaxton Paramount 3500 III	C49FT	1991	
J62NTM	Mercedes-Benz 0303/15	Plaxton Paramount 3500 III	C53F	1992	
K436AVS	Plaxton 425	Lorraine	C55F	1993	
L372LHE	Scania K113CRB	Van Hool Alizee HE	C53F	1994	
L373LHE	Scania K113CRB	Van Hool Alizee HE	C53F	1994	
N686AHL	Scania K93CRB	Berkhof Excellence 1000 L	C55F	1995	
P131GHE	Scania K113CRB	Van Hool Alizee HE	C53F	1997	

Livery:- White with red relief. K436AVS carries ISS fleetnames.

SEE-MORE TRAVEL

R.E. Horn, 5a Sedgemere Avenue, East Finchley, London, N2 0SY

Previous Owner

VBY793L	AEC Reliance 6U3ZR	Plaxton Panorama Elite III	C53F	1973	Galleon, Stratford, 1982
112VMV	AEC Reliance 6U3ZR	Plaxton Supreme III	C45F	1976	Layland, Torquay, 1989
FME80V	Volvo B58-61	Plaxton Supreme IV	C57F	1980	Ming, Harringay, 1987
B58VMJ	Ford Transit	Dixon Lomas	M12	1984	Burton, Finchley, 1994

Previous Registrations:-

VBY793L OMH496L, 112VMV
112VMV LME413P

Livery:- White with yellow, blue and green relief.

SIDCUP COACHES

N.B. D'Cruze, 91 Langford Place, Sidcup, Kent, DA14 4AZ

Previous Owner

PPE664R	Bedford YMT	Duple Dominant II	C53F	1977	Palmer, Bromley, 1990
APW276S	Leyland Leopard PSU5B/4R	Duple Dominant II	C53F	1977	Floyd, Orpington, 1993
AYJ987T	Bedford YMT	Duple Dominant II	C53F	1979	White-Hyde & Bowen, Rye, 1992
EGY619T	Bedford YMT	Duple Dominant II	C53F	1979	Dashminster, Bromley, 1992
NKN448W	Ford Transit	Ford	M14	1981	private owner, 1992
MFS390X	Leyland Leopard PSU5C/4R	Duple Dominant IV	C49FT	1982	Romney, Hillingdon, 1997
G787VJU	Leyland-DAF 400	Leyland-DAF	M16	1989	M.Track, Crayford, 1997

Previous Registrations:- **APW276S** WUG151S, 123SRT   **EGY619T** BGY599T, CIB926   **MFS390X** PWB658X, YFG333

Livery:- Various.

SILVERDALE

Croxmead Ltd, Atlas Road, North Acton, London, NW10 6WD

Previous Owner

LDZ2948	Volvo B10M-61	Plaxton Paramount 3500 II	C53F	1985	Silverdale, Nottingham, 1996
J724CWT	Volvo B10M-60	Plaxton Premiere 350	C48FT	1992	Wallace Arnold, 1997
K101UFP	Volvo B10M-60	Caetano Algarve II	C53F	1993	Silverdale, Nottingham, 1996
K102UFP	Volvo B10M-60	Caetano Algarve II	C53F	1993	Silverdale, Nottingham, 1994
L545XUT	Toyota Coaster HZB50R	Caetano Optimo III	C21F	1994	Silverdale, Nottingham, 1994
M939JJU	Volvo B10M-62	Plaxton Premiere 350	C49FT	1995	Silverdale, Nottingham, 1997
N127RJF	Volvo B10M-62	Plaxton Premiere 350	C53F	1996	

Previous Registration:- **LDZ2948** B634OFP

Livery:- Yellow with black and red relief.   Special Livery:- N127RJF is in Network Europa Travel livery.

SILVERGRAY

P.A. Ward, J.C. Silverwood & V.J. Keith, Bedfont Trading Estate, Bedfont Road, Bedfont, Middlesex, TW14 8EE

Previous Owner

CAZ2050	Volvo B10M-61	Van Hool Astral	CH6/6FT	1984	Showline, Abercynon, 1993
FIL9372	DAF SBR2300DHS570	Jonckheere Jubilee P99	CH9/7DT	1985	Falcon, Kentish Town,1994
C275LBH	Volvo B10M-61	Van Hool Alizee H	C10FT	1986	Hallmark, Luton, 1996
JAZ9420	DAF SBR2300DHS570	Van Hool Astrobel	CH8/8CT	1987	Wharfedale, Nuneaton, 1996
D920BGM	Volvo B10M-61	Van Hool Astral	CH7/7FT	1988	GZ Touring, Den Haag, 1996
E656KCX	DAF SBR2300DHS570	Van Hool Astrobel	CH8/8CT	1988	Berryhurst, Lambeth, 1995
L543XUT	Toyota Coaster HDB30R	Caetano Optimo II	C18F	1994	A & R, Bedfont, 1997

Note:- D920BGM is left hand drive.

All the fleet is generally employed on touring with bands, usually abroad, and consequently fitted out as mobile hotels thus:-

C275LBH	10 bunks	D920BGM	13 bunks
CAZ2050	12 bunks	FIL9372, E656KCX, JAZ9420	16 bunks.

Previous Registrations:-

CAZ2050	A549XUH	**JAZ9420**	D132ACX	**C275LBH**	C238GBH, MSK286	**D920BGM**	BV-35-ZX	**FIL9372**	B499GBD

Livery:- Silver with blue signwriting

SILVERWING

Aviation Defence International Ground Services Ltd, 120 Bath Road, Heathrow, Middlesex, UB3 5AN   *Previous Owner*

	OGN877Y	Leyland National 2 NL106TL11/2R			B31F	1983	Speedlink, 1995
	A544WGP	Leyland National 2 NL106TL11/2R			B31D	1984	Speedlink, 1995
	A545WGP	Leyland National 2 NL106TL11/2R			B31D	1984	Speedlink, 1995
	A546WGP	Leyland National 2 NL106TL11/2R			B31D	1984	Speedlink, 1995
	B360LOY	Leyland National 2 NL116TL11/3R			B33DO	1984	British Airways, 1996
	B361LOY	Leyland National 2 NL116TL11/3R			DP40DO	1984	British Airways, 1996
	B362LOY	Leyland National 2 NL116TL11/3R			B33DO	1984	British Airways, 1996
	C904VLB	Dodge G10	Wadham Stringer Vanguard	B29F	1985	British Airways, 1995
	C913VLB	Dodge G13	Wadham Stringer Vanguard	DP39F	1986	British Airways, 1995
	D48YLH	Volkswagen Transporter	Advanced Vehicle Builders	M8	1987	AMR, Bedfont, 1995
22	F587OHM	Volkswagen Transporter	Volkswagen	M8	1988	AMR, Bedfont, 1995
	G362YLT	Mercedes-Benz 609D	Devon Conversions	B20F	1989	private owner, 1996
23	G587UYL	Volkswagen Transporter	Volkswagen	M7	1990	private owner, 1995
26	G164XJF	Toyota Coaster HB31R	Caetano Optimo	C18F	1990	Scancoaches, North Acton, 1995
25	H204NFX	Toyota Coaster HDB30R	Caetano Optimo II	C21F	1991	Budden, Romsey, 1995
27	H187EJF	Toyota Coaster HDB30R	Caetano Optimo II	C18F	1991	Marchwood, Totton, 1995
24	H261FPD	Mercedes-Benz 609D	Crystals	C23F	1991	AMR, Bedfont, 1995
	K658VNF	Mercedes-Benz 711D	Made To Measure	C24F	1992	Corton, Ashton-under-Lyne, 1996
28	K809EET	Toyota Coaster HDB30R	Caetano Optimo II	C21F	1993	Hudson, Bilbrough, 1995
29	M683DGN	LDV 400	LDV	M16	1995	private owner, 1995
	M785VJO	Dennis Javelin 12SDA2146	Caetano Algarve II	C49FT	1995	D & J, Silvertown, 1997
	N789VBL	Volkswagen Caravelle	Volkswagen	M7	1995	Whites, Ascot (dealer),1995
	N206VJB	Volkswagen Caravelle	Volkswagen	M11	1995	
	N207VJB	Volkswagen Caravelle	Volkswagen	M11	1995	
	N239VJB	Volkswagen Caravelle	Volkswagen	M7	1995	
01	N469VJH	Citroen Relay	Citroen	M11	1995	
02	N470VJH	Citroen Relay	Citroen	M11	1995	
04	N471VJH	Citroen Relay	Citroen	M11	1995	

	Reg	Model	Body	Seating	Year	Notes
09	N472VJH	Citroen Relay	Citroen	M11	1995	
	N473VJH	Citroen Relay	Citroen	M11	1995	
05	N474VJH	Citroen Relay	Citroen	M11	1995	
	N475VJH	Citroen Relay	Citroen	M11	1995	
08	N476VJH	Citroen Relay	Citroen	M11	1995	
18	N478VJH	Citroen Relay	Citroen	M11	1995	
06	N479VJH	Citroen Relay	Citroen	M11	1995	
07	N480VJH	Citroen Relay	Citroen	M11	1995	
11	N482VJH	Citroen Relay	Citroen	M11	1995	
	N483VJH	Citroen Relay	Citroen	M11	1995	
12	N484VJH	Citroen Relay	Citroen	M11	1995	
19	N485VJH	Citroen Relay	Citroen	M11	1995	
	N486VJH	Citroen Relay	Citroen	M11	1995	
	N487VJH	Citroen Relay	Citroen	M11	1995	
	N581GBW	Dennis Javelin 12SDA2147	Caetano Algarve II	C53F	1995	On loan from Dawson Rentals
	N512ENK	Ford Transit	Ford	M8	1996	
	N270HGO	LDV 400	LDV	M16	1996	
	N592TAY	Iveco ECO3.CC.95	Indcar 80	C35F	1996	
	N593TAY	Iveco ECO3.CC.95	Indcar 80	C35F	1996	
	N594TAY	Iveco ECO3.CC.95	Indcar 80	C35F	1996	
	N595TAY	Iveco ECO3.CC.95	Indcar 80	C35F	1996	

	Volvo B6LE-53	Wright Crusader	B21FO	1996
N241WRW	N242WRW	N243WRW	N244WRW	N245WRW	N246WRW

	Reg	Model	Body	Seating	Year
	N157YMO	Volkswagen Caravelle	Trimtruck	M7	1996
	N158YMO	Volkswagen Caravelle	Trimtruck	M7	1996
	P712EGM	Volkswagon Transporter	Trimtruck	M7	1997

	Dennis Dart SLF SFD322BR1TGW1	UVG Urbanstar SLF	B34FO	1997
P81MOR	P82MOR	P910MOR	P503MOT	P504MOT	P505MOT

	Reg	Model	Body	Seating	Year	Notes
	P428PBP	Dennis Javelin SFD721BR3VGJ2	UVG S320	C57F	1997	On loan from UVG
	P218VGN	LDV Convoy	LDV	M16	1997	
	P219VGN	LDV Convoy	LDV	M16	1997	

Note:- DO and FO after seating capacity denote additional door/s fitted to offside.

Previous Registrations:- **H204NFX**   H387CFT, SJI8128

Livery:- White with blue signwriting.   Special Liveries:- British Midland:- OGN877Y, A544-6WGP, N241-4WRW.

SIMMONDS

I.D. Kirton, 31 Ashford Avenue, Hayes, Middlesex, UB4 0LZ

					Previous Owner
LAH815A	AEC Reliance 2U3RA	Plaxton Panorama Elite II (1972)	C49F	1962	Caroline Seagull, Great Yarmouth, 1994
SXD475F	Leyland Panther PSUR1/2RT	Plaxton Panorama	C51F	1968	Isleworth, Twickenham, 1975
JGW184N	Bedford YRT	Duple Dominant	C53F	1975	Lawrence, Hillingdon, 1994
LPB118P	Volvo B58-61	Duple Dominant	C53F	1976	Crawley Luxury, 1989
LRX831P	AEC Reliance 6U3ZR	Plaxton Supreme III	C51F	1976	Horseman, Reading, 1997
HIL5875	Leyland Leopard PSU3C/4R	Plaxton Supreme III	C53F	1976	Hearn, Harrow Weald, 1995
UPK131S	Leyland Atlantean AN68A/1R	Park Royal	H43/30F	1978	Red & Green, Chislehurst, 1994
TND122X	Volvo B58-61	Duple Dominant IV	C53F	1982	Southern Vectis, 1991
TND131X	Volvo B58-61	Duple Dominant IV	C53F	1982	Southern Vectis, 1991
D589VBV	Freight-Rover Sherpa	Dormobile	B16F	1986	West London, Tylers Green, 1997

Previous Registrations:- **HIL5875** MKJ252P   **LAH815A** 537FN   **LUY321N** KAB400N, HYY3

Livery:- Various

SKINNERS

S.M.N. & D.M. Skinner, 15 Barrow Green Road, Oxted, Surrey, RH8 0NJ

					Previous Owner
661SKN	Bedford YMT	Plaxton Supreme IV	C53F	1979	
798SKN	Bedford YMT	Plaxton Supreme IV	C53F	1979	
6SKN	Kassbohrer Setra S215HD	Kassbohrer Optimal	C49FT	1983	
SKN418	Kassbohrer Setra S215H	Kassbohrer Optimal	C53F	1984	
B883AGJ	Mercedes-Benz L307D	Devon Conversions	M12	1985	
182SKN	Mercedes-Benz L608D	Robin Hood	C19F	1985	
435SKN	Kassbohrer Setra S210HD	Kassbohrer Optimal	C35FT	1986	
837SKN	Mercedes-Benz 307D	Reeve Burgess	M12	1987	
H330KCF	Dennis Javelin 11SDL1921	Duple 320	C55F	1991	private owner, 1992
J872RPJ	MCW Metrorider MF156	MCW	C25F	1992	
747SKN	Kassbohrer Setra S250	Kassbohrer Special	C48FT	1996	
P980HWF	Dennis Javelin SFD532BR3TGJ6	Auwaerter Transliner	C53F	1997	

Named Vehicles:- SKN418, 6SKN, 435SKN Skinners Europa Bus   P980HWF Skinners European

Previous Registrations:-

SKN418	A725HPF	**435SKN**	C855UPM	**798SKN**	HRO447V	**837SKN**	D676CPF, 747SKN
6SKN	YPG974Y	**661SKN**	CMJ443T				
182SKN	B489CGN						

Livery:- Fawn with brown relief.

SPIRIT OF LONDON

Elitemart Ltd, 22 Browning Way, Heston, Middlesex, TW5 5BE   *Previous Owner*

GIL8497	Volvo B10M-61	Berkhof Esprite 350	C49FT	1987	Kingston Coaches, Winterslow, 1996
GIL8498	Volvo B10M-61	Berkhof Esprite 350	C49FT	1987	Kingston Coaches, Winterslow, 1996
TJI3131	Van Hool T815H	Van Hool Alizee H	C49FT	1990	Dick, Dorney, 1996

Previous Registrations:- **GIL8497** E234AVX   **GIL8498** E235AVX   **TJI3131** G431VML

Liveries:- White (GIL8497/8) or red (TJI3131)

STARLINE

J.P. Mullany, Clarendon Garage, Cardiff Road, Watford, Hertfordshire, WD1 8DG   *Previous Owner*

DM2143	OJD143R	Leyland Fleetline FE30AGR	Park Royal	H45/27D	1976	London Buses, 1990
DM2411	OJD411R	Leyland Fleetline FE30ALR	Park Royal	H44/24D	1977	Bryan's, Enfield, 1994
	KBC3V	Volvo B58-61	Plaxton Supreme IV	C57F	1980	P & J Ellis, Wembley Park, 1987
	YDN504	Mercedes-Benz L307D	Reeve Burgess	M12	1983	Simmonds, Letchworth, 1989
	EBZ6294	Volvo B10M-61	Duple Laser	C57F	1983	Link Line, Harlesden, 1987
	EBZ6295	Volvo B10M-61	Plaxton Paramount 3500	C57F	1983	Skill, Nottingham, 1989
	EBZ6296	Volvo B10M-61	Plaxton Paramount 3500	C57F	1983	Skill, Sheffield, 1989
T896	A896SYE	Leyland Titan TNLXB2RRSp	Leyland	H44/27D	1983	London United, 1996
	FDZ4730	Volvo B10M-61	Van Hool Alizee H	C53F	1984	Shearings, 1990
	FDZ5348	Volvo B10M-61	Van Hool Alizee H	C53F	1984	Shearings, 1991
	B21CYS	Mercedes-Benz L307D	Reeve Burgess	M12	1985	Barrett, Great Mongeham, 1992
	C938RPK	Mercedes-Benz L608D	Coachcraft	C21F	1986	
	C518DND	Volvo B10M-61	Plaxton Paramount 3200 II	C53F	1986	Brents, Watford, 1997
	FDZ3715	Scania K112CRS	Van Hool Alizee SH	C51FT	1987	TRJ, Golborne, 1994
	E41MMT	Mercedes-Benz 609D	Reeve Burgess	B20F	1987	
	E219JJF	Volvo B10M-61	Van Hool Alizee	C53F	1988	Clarkes, Sydenham, 1997
	F796FKU	Mercedes-Benz 811D	Whittaker	C24F	1989	
	G870MAH	Volvo B10M-60	Plaxton Paramount 3500 III	C53F	1989	The Londoners, Nunhead, 1996
	H254LOX	Mercedes-Benz 709D	Blytheswood (1994)	C16FL	1991	private owner, 1994
	M669UCT	Mercedes-Benz 814D	Autobus Classique	C33F	1995	

Previous Registrations:-

YDN504 HBH402Y   **EBZ6295** YNN31Y   **FDZ3715** D910RBU   **FDZ5348** A180MNE
EBZ6294 MSU598Y, EJV248, FLB453Y   **EBZ6296** YNN30Y   **FDZ4730** A179MNE

Named Vehicle:- KBC3V   The North Star

Livery:- White (YDN504 & B21CYS) or white with blue relief.   Special Livery:- FDZ3715 is white with gold relief.

SUNBURY COACHES

Sunbury Coaches Ltd, 74 Kenyngton Drive, Sunbury-on-Thames, Middlesex, TW16 7RX   *Previous Owner*

DJF632T	Bedford YMT	Plaxton Supreme IV	C53F	1979	Jones, Laleham, 1988
HIL6754	Volvo B10M-61	Jonckheere Jubilee P599	C53F	1983	Dodsworth, Boroughbridge, 1994
NYS58Y	Leyland Tiger TRCTL11/3R	Van Hool Alizee H	C52F	1983	Mitchell, Plean, 1994
B339AMH	Leyland Tiger TRCTL11/3R	Van Hool Alizee H	C53F	1985	Worthing Coaches, 1991
B125KPF	Leyland Tiger TRCTL11/3RH	Berkhof Everest 370	C53F	1985	Northumbria, 1993

Named Vehicles:- B339AMH   William Jones   HIL6754   Vernon Goslin

Previous Registration:- **HIL6754** A307XHE

Livery:- White, turquoise and navy blue.

SWALLOW COACH COMPANY

Swallow Coach Company Ltd, Rainham House, Manor Way, Rainham, Essex, RM13 8RE   *Previous Owner*

8056UA	Leyland Leopard PSU3B/4R	Willowbrook Crusader (1990)	C53F	1972	Bygone, Biddenden, 1994
FAA757S	Volvo B58-56	Plaxton Supreme III	C53F	1977	non PSV, 1995
NIW5984	Volvo B58-61	Jonckheere Bermuda	C49FT	1979	Goodwin, Eccles, 1995
JIL5287	Ford R1114	Plaxton Supreme IV Express	C53F	1980	Bolton, Farnham, 1990
JIL5288	Leyland Leopard PSU3E/4R	Plaxton Supreme IV Express	C48F	1981	United Counties, 1990
KIJ4783	Kassbohrer Setra S215H	Kassbohrer Optimal	C50F	1981	Pullen & Taylor, Titchfield, 1996
Q201SDS	Leyland Leopard PSU3F/5R	Willowbrook Warrior (1991)	B51F	1982	Henderson, Hamilton, 1996
UAU227X	DAF MB200DKTL600	Plaxton Supreme V	C52F	1982	Oakfield, Enfield, 1991
448DAE	Mercedes-Benz 0303/15R	Jonckheere Jubilee P50	C49FT	1983	Anderson, Bermondsey, 1995
C174KET	Auwaerter Neoplan N122/3	Auwaerter Skyliner	CH57/20CT	1986	Yorkshire Voyager,1992
JIL4314	Volvo B10M-53	Van Hool Alizee SH	C49FT	1986	Gardiner, East Kilbride, 1997
D871NVS	Freight Rover Sherpa 374	Dormobile	B16F	1986	Powney, Aintree, 1990
E565YBU	Mercedes-Benz 709D	Reeve Burgess Beaver	B19F	1988	Star Line, Knutsford, 1993
GIL3270	DAF SB3000DKV601	Caetano Algarve	C49FT	1989	Wilson, Carnwath, 1994
F200THK	Sanos S315.21	FAP Charisma	C49FT	1989	Ford Motor Co., Warley, 1997
F203XBV	Freight-Rover Sherpa	Carlyle Citybus 2	B20F	1989	ABC, Ainsdale, 1997
F888SMU	Volvo B10M-61	Van Hool Alizee H	C49FT	1989	
G650LWF	Volvo B10M-60	Ikarus Blue Danube 336	C53FT	1989	
K11WEB	Toyota Coaster HDB30R	Caetano Optimo II	C21F	1992	Wheadon, Cardiff, 1995
L41CNY	Volvo B10M-60	Plaxton Premiere 350	C53F	1993	Bebb, Llantwit Fardre, 1997
L56DNY	Volvo B10M-60	Plaxton Premiere 320	C49FT	1993	Bebb, Llantwit Fardre, 1997
M6WEB	Volvo B10M-62	Caetano Algarve II	C49FT	1995	

N6WEB	MAN 18.370	Caetano Algarve III	C53F	1996
P6WEB	Volvo B10MSE-62	Jonckheere Mistral 50	C53F	1996
P7WEB	Volvo B10MSE-62	Jonckheere Mistral 50	C51FT	1996

Named Vehicles:-

C174KET	Gemma	F888SMU	Tricky Ricky	M6WEB	Kelly Anne
448DAE	Billy Ben	K11WEB	Little Luke	N6WEB	Lucky Lee
E205EPB	Crafty Carl	KIJ4783	Tommy	P7WEB	Gillian

Previous Registrations:-

448DAE	From new
GIL3270	F207PNR
JIL4314	C362KGG, D574NNS
JIL5287	NVT 452W
JIL5288	MAP344W, XLD244, OUF56W
K11WEB	K202PNR
KIJ4783	FTP137X
NIW5984	GMJ837T, 7CCH, UEY51T, HPV849, SWH133T
Q201SDS	50 AC 01
8056UA	YDF323K

Livery:- White or white and blue. (P6/7WEB are metallic turquoise)

TWH TRAVEL

TWH Travel Ltd, 14 Devoil Close, Burpham, Surrey, GU4 7FG

					Previous Owner
F704PAY	Mercedes-Benz 0303/15R	Mercedes-Benz	C53F	1989	Redwing, Camberwell, 1996
F706PAY	Mercedes-Benz 0303/15R	Mercedes-Benz	C53F	1989	Redwing, Camberwell, 1996
L51LTF	Bova FHD12.290	Bova Futura	C49FT	1994	Bennett, Chieveley, 1997

Previous Registration:-

| **L51LTF** | L5BSL |

Liveries:- Red and cream (F704PAY), white, dark green and gold (F706PAY) or green (L51LTF)

TELLINGS-GOLDEN MILLER

Tellings-Golden Miller Ltd, 20a Wintersells Road, Byfleet, Surrey, KT14 7LF

Previous Owner

						Previous Owner
	DKX111X	Volvo B10M-61	Plaxton Supreme IV	C57F	1982	Link Line, Harlesden, 1994
	A388XMC	Volvo B10M-61	Plaxton Paramount 3500	C53F	1984	Sheenway, Sheen, 1991
	B731YUD	Ford Transit 190D	Carlyle	B20F	1985	Buslink, Stubwood, 1995
	B737YUD	Ford Transit 190D	Carlyle	B20F	1985	Stevensons, 1995
	C669XRU	Volvo B10M-61	Plaxton Paramount 3500 II	C53F	1986	Sheenway, Sheen, 1991
	D141TMR	Mercedes-Benz L307D	Whittaker	M12	1987	Stone, Wilton, 1997
803	E224PWY	MCW Metrorider MF150/34	MCW	DP23F	1987	Stevensons, 1994
802	E232PWY	MCW Metrorider MF150/41	MCW	B23F	1987	Cardiff Bluebird, 1995
804	E804UDT	MCW Metrorider MF150/15	MCW	B23F	1987	Stevensons, 1994
808	E808UDT	MCW Metrorider MF150/15	MCW	B23F	1987	Cardiff Bluebird, 1995
805	E604VKC	MCW Metrorider MF150/40	MCW	B23F	1987	Cardiff Bluebird, 1995
	E460ANC	Mercedes-Benz 507D	Made To Measure	M16	1988	Spirit of London, Hounslow, 1996
801	F101YVP	MCW Metrorider MF150/115	MCW	B25F	1988	Cardiff Bluebird, 1996
	F71SJX	Mercedes-Benz 709D	Onyx	DP24F	1989	South Lancs, St Helens, 1996
	TFA13	Volkswagen Caravelle	Volkswagen	M7	1990	KF Cars, Gatwick, 1995
	H120YGG	Mercedes-Benz 709D	Dormobile	B27F	1990	Goosecroft, Stirling, 1997
	L10TGM	Volvo B10M-62	Jonckheere Deauville 45L	C51FT	1994	
	L20TGM	Volvo B10M-62	Jonckheere Deauville 45L	C51FT	1994	
	M10TGM	Volvo B10M-62	Jonckheere Deauville 45L	C51FT	1994	
	M20TGM	Volvo B10M-62	Jonckheere Deauville 45L	C51FT	1994	
	M30TGM	Dennis Javelin 12SDA2131	Plaxton Premiere 320	C57F	1995	
	M40TGM	Dennis Javelin 12SDA2155	Plaxton Premiere 320	C57F	1995	
	M50TGM	Dennis Javelin 12SDA2155	Plaxton Premiere 320	C53F	1995	
	M60TGM	Toyota Coaster HZB50R	Caetano Optimo III	C18F	1995	
	M70TGM	Mercedes-Benz 709D	Plaxton Beaver	B23F	1995	
	M80TGM	Mercedes-Benz 709D	Plaxton Beaver	B23F	1995	
	M90TGM	Mercedes-Benz 709D	Plaxton Beaver	B23F	1995	
	N60TGM	Toyota Coaster HZB50R	Caetano Optimo III	C21F	1995	
	N956DWJ	Volvo B10M-62	Plaxton Premiere 350	C49FT	1996	
	N957DWJ	Volvo B10M-62	Plaxton Premiere 350	C49FT	1996	
	N20GTA	Volvo B10M-62	Plaxton Premiere 350	C53F	1996	
	N30GTA	Volvo B10M-62	Plaxton Premiere 350	C53F	1996	
	N10TGM	Volvo B10M-62	Van Hool Alizee HE	C32FT	1996	
	N20TGM	Volvo B10M-62	Van Hool Alizee HE	C48FT	1996	
	N30TGM	Dennis Javelin 12SDA2155	Plaxton Premiere 320	C57F	1996	
	N40TGM	Dennis Javelin 12SDA2155	Plaxton Premiere 320	C57F	1996	
	N50TGM	Volvo B10M-62	Plaxton Premiere 350	C53F	1996	
	N70TGM	Mercedes-Benz 709D	Plaxton Beaver	B23F	1996	

N80TGM	Volvo B10M-62	Van Hool Alizee HE	C48FT	1996	
N90TGM	Volvo B10M-62	Van Hool Alizee HE	C48FT	1996	
P200GTA	Volvo B10M-62	Plaxton Premiere 350	C53F	1997	
P300GTA	Volvo B10M-62	Plaxton Premiere 350	C53F	1997	
P10TGM	Volvo B10M-62	Van Hool Alizee HE	C32FT	1997	
P20TGM	Volvo B10M-62	Plaxton Premiere 350	C48FT	1997	
P30TGM	Volvo B10M-62	Plaxton Premiere 350	C48FT	1997	
P40TGM	Mercedes-Benz 814D	Plaxton Beaver	C33F	1997	
P50TGM	Mercedes-Benz 814D	Plaxton Beaver	C33F	1997	
P70TGM	Mercedes-Benz 709D	Plaxton Beaver	B27F	1997	
	Mercedes-Benz Vario 0.814D	Plaxton Beaver II	B31F	1997	

701 P701LCF   702 P702LCF   703 P703LCF   704 P704LCF   705 R705MJH   706 R706MJH

On Order:- 14 x Dennis Dart SLF/Plaxton Pointer II for December 1997 delivery for LT tendered route 235.

Previous Registrations:- **TFA13** G504DDP   **DKX111X** VCX411X, 403NMM

Livery:- White, blue and yellow.

Special Liveries:-

Executive livery (Gold and blue):- N10TGM, P10TGM.
Grand European Tours (White with red and blue relief):- N956DWJ, N957DWJ.
Gullivers Travel Agency (White and blue):- N20GTA, N30GTA.
Gullivers Travel Agency (Blue with white fleetnames):- P200GTA, P300GTA.

EDWARD THOMAS & SON

Ivan Edward Thomas, 442 Chessington Road, West Ewell, Surrey, KT19 9EJ   *Previous Owner*

GUD708L	Leyland Leopard PSU3B/4R	Plaxton Panorama Elite III	C51F	1972	Charlton Services, Charlton-on-Otmoor, 1996
RJI5710	AEC Reliance 6U2R	Plaxton Supreme III	C57F	1977	Brijan Tours, Swanmore, 1995
LTK91R	Leyland Atlantean AN68A/1R	Roe	H43/29F	1977	Finglands, Manchester, 1997
LTK94R	Leyland Atlantean AN68A/1R	Roe	H43/29F	1977	Finglands, Manchester, 1997
435UPD	AEC Reliance 6U3ZR	Plaxton Supreme III	C53F	1978	
YPL63T	AEC Reliance 6U2R	Duple Dominant II Express	C49F	1979	Ken's, Peckham, 1997
267PPH	Leyland Leopard PSU5C/4R	Plaxton Supreme IV	C57F	1979	Frames Rickards, Brentford, 1986
VJY139V	Leyland Atlantean AN68A/1R	East Lancashire	H43/28D	1980	Plymouth Citybus, 1996
VJY141V	Leyland Atlantean AN68A/1R	East Lancashire	H43/28D	1980	Plymouth Citybus, 1996
160CLT	Leyland Tiger TRCTL11/3R	Plaxton Supreme V	C53F	1982	London Country North West, 1989
HIL4017	Leyland Tiger TRCTL11/2R	Plaxton Supreme V	C53F	1982	

GAC97Y	Leyland Tiger TRCTL11/3R	Plaxton Paramount 3500	C53F	1983	A & D, Worcester Park, 1997
HIL3207	Leyland Tiger TRCTL11/3R	Plaxton Paramount 3200	C53F	1983	
A518LPP	Leyland Tiger TRCTL11/3R	Plaxton Paramount 3200	C53F	1983	Frames Rickards, Brentford, 1989
H312HPF	Leyland Tiger TRCTL11/3R	Van Hool Alizee (1990)	C53F	1983	MOD, 1990 (Chassis Only)
A51GPG	Leyland Tiger TRCTL11/3R	Plaxton Paramount 3200	C53F	1984	
C913UPB	Leyland Tiger TRCTL11/3R	Plaxton Paramount 3200	C53F	1986	

Previous Registrations:-

HIL3207	APJ445Y	**RJI5710**	OEB693R	**267PPH**	KBH842V	**GAC97Y**	WWA303Y, 3063VC
HIL4017	UPE755X	**160CLT**	SMY629X	**435UPD**	WPJ455S	**H312HPF**	20KB76

Livery:- Two tone green and cream or green and cream.

THORPES

F.E. Thorpe & Sons Ltd, 272 Latimer Road, North Kensington, London, W10 6QY   *Previous Owner*

C118EMG	Volvo B10M-61	Plaxton Paramount 3200 II	C48FT	1985	Horseshoe, Kempston, 1991
TIB8571	Volvo B10M-61	Jonckheere Jubilee P599	C51FT	1987	Scancoaches, North Acton, 1996
E157KDP	Volvo B10M-61 (Shortened)	Plaxton Paramount 3200 III	C43F	1987	Ralph's, Langley, 1994
E29WGJ	Mercedes-Benz 709D	Pilcher-Greene	C18FL	1987	Police Convalescent Home, Goring, 1987
LBZ2938	Volvo B10M-61	Plaxton Paramount 3500 III	C53F	1988	Ralph's, Langley, 1996
F823MRX	Freight-Rover Sherpa	Freight-Rover	M16	1988	McCouid, Burghfield, 1997
G822UMU	Volvo B10M-61	Plaxton Paramount 3500 III	C53F	1989	
J11ALP	Auwaerter Neoplan N208	Auwaerter Jetliner	C24FT	1992	Dereham Coachways, East Dereham, 1997
J839KNL	Leyland-DAF 400	Autobus Classique	C16F	1992	Jones, Newton Aycliffe, 1994
K4FET	Mercedes-Benz 814D	Plaxton Beaver	C33F	1993	
K53TER	Volvo B10M-62	Van Hool Alizee	C53F	1993	Kenzies, Shepreth, 1996

Named Vehicle:- G822UMU   Jim & Frank.

Previous Registrations:- **LBZ2938**   E580UHS   **TIB8571**   D97BNV   **E157KDP**   WSV468

Livery:- Yellow and white (J11ALP is gold).

The vehicles employed on LT services are shown in the *London Bus Handbook*.

TRANSYLVANIAN EXPRESS

D. Silman, 57 Mellitus Street, East Acton, London, W12 0AU   *Previous Owner*

A408GPY	Kassbohrer Setra S228DT	Kassbohrer Imperial	CH54/20DT	1984	Harmer, Bexhill, 1996

Livery:- Multicoloured

TRAVELLERS

Brelaton Ltd, Unit C1, Tamian Way, Hounslow, Middlesex, TW4 6BL

Reg	Chassis	Body	Layout	Year			
H433GVL	Kassbohrer Setra S215HR	Kassbohrer Rational	C53F	1991			
H434GVL	Kassbohrer Setra S215HR	Kassbohrer Rational	C53F	1991			
J1TCC	Kassbohrer Setra S215HD	Kassbohrer Tornado	C49FT	1992			
J4TCC	Kassbohrer Setra S215HD	Kassbohrer Tornado	C49FT	1992			
K1TCC	Kassbohrer Setra S215HD	Kassbohrer Tornado	C28FT	1992			
M20TCC	Volvo B12T	Jonckheere Monaco	CH57/14CT	1994			
M20BUS	Dennis Javelin 12SDA2159	Plaxton Premiere 350	C53F	1995			
M40TCC	Kassbohrer Setra S250	Kassbohrer Special	C48FT	1995			
M50TCC	Kassbohrer Setra S250	Kassbohrer Special	C48FT	1995			
M60TCC	Toyota Coaster HZB50R	Caetano Optimo III	C18F	1995			
M70TCC	Toyota Coaster HZB50R	Caetano Optimo III	C18F	1995			
M80TCC	Toyota Coaster HZB50R	Caetano Optimo III	C18F	1995			
	Dennis Javelin 12SDA2159	Plaxton Premiere 350	C53F	1996			
N10TCC	N20TCC	N30TCC	N40TCC	N50TCC			
N60TCC	Toyota Coaster HZB50R	Caetano Optimo III	C18F	1996			
N70TCC	Toyota Coaster HZB50R	Caetano Optimo III	C18F	1996			
N80TCC	Toyota Coaster HZB50R	Caetano Optimo III	C18F	1996			
N100TCC	Kassbohrer Setra S250	Kassbohrer Special	C53F	1996			
N200TCC	Kassbohrer Setra S250	Kassbohrer Special	C53F	1996			
N300TCC	Kassbohrer Setra S250	Kassbohrer Special	C57F	1996			
N400TCC	Kassbohrer Setra S250	Kassbohrer Special	C57F	1996			
N500TCC	Volvo B10M-62	Plaxton Premiere 350	C48F	1996			
N600TCC	Volvo B10M-62	Plaxton Premiere 350	C48F	1996			
P10TCC	Auwaerter Neoplan N122/3	Auwaerter Skyliner	CH57/20DT	1996			
P200OMT	Kassbohrer Setra S250	Kassbohrer Special	C32FT	1997			
	Dennis Javelin SFD731BR3TGJ4	Plaxton Premiere 350	C53F	1997			
P22TCC	P55TCC	P77TCC	P88TCC	P99TCC	P222TCC	P333TCC	
P44TCC	P66TCC						
P33TCC	Dennis Javelin SFD731BR3TVGJ4	Plaxton Premiere 350	C53F	1997			

	Kassbohrer Setra S250		Kassbohrer Special	C48F	1997		
P100TCC	P200TCC	P400TCC	P600TCC	P700TCC		P800TCC	P900TCC
P111TCC	P300TCC	P500TCC					

P444TCC	Dennis Javelin SFD731BR3TGJ2	Plaxton Premiere 320	C51F	1997	
P555TCC	Dennis Javelin SFD731BR3TGJ2	Plaxton Premiere 320	C51F	1997	
P666TCC	Dennis Javelin SFD731BR3TGJ2	Plaxton Premiere 320	C51F	1997	
P777TCC	Dennis Javelin SFD731BR3TGJ2	Plaxton Premiere 320	C51F	1997	

Previous registrations:-

J1TCC J7TCC **P10TCC** P981HWF **P111TCC** P137XFW **P200OMT** P693XVL **P400TCC** P691XVL

Named Vehicles:- K1TCC The Diplomat P200OMT The Millennium Traveller

Livery:- Silver with red, white and blue relief.

Special liveries:-

Cosmos(white with red signwriting):-	P444TCC, P555TCC, P666TCC, P777TCC
Globus (white & red) :-	N500TCC, N600TCC, P100TCC, P111TCC, P200TCC, P300TCC,
	P400TCC, P500TCC, P600TCC, P700TCC, P800TCC, P900TCC
My Bus (white with red and grey signwriting):-	M20BUS, P222TCC, P333TCC.

TRINA TOURS

Trina Tours Ltd, 74 New Oxford Street, Holborn, London, WC1A 1EU

G170XJF	Toyota Coaster HB31R	Caetano Optimo	C18F	1990
K810EET	Volvo B10M-60	Van Hool Alizee HE	C31FT	1992
K420JWB	Volvo B10M-60	Van Hool Alizee HE	C53F	1993
M573JBC	Volvo B10M-62	Caetano Algarve II	C51F	1995
N236NNR	Volvo B10M-62	Caetano Algarve II	C51FT	1995
N967DME	Ford Transit	Ford	M8	1996
N968DME	Ford Transit	Ford	M8	1996
P963DNR	Toyota Coaster BB50R	Caetano Optimo IV	C18F	1997

Livery:- Silver and black.

TROIKA TRAVEL

D.J. Lock, 11 Freelands Avenue, Monks Hill, Croydon, Surrey, CR2 8HT   *Previous Owner*

YJM355T	DAF MB200DKL550	Plaxton Supreme IV	C53F	1979	Melsway, Kings Cross, 1996
F823LRS	DAF SB3000DKV601	Van Hool Alizee H	C55F	1989	Burns, Tarves, 1996

Named Vehicle:-   F823LRS   Royal Queen

Previous Registration:- **F823LRS** F658OHD, YSU922

Livery:- White (YJM355T) or white with orange and yellow relief (F823LRS).

VENTURE

Venture Transport (Hendon) (1965) Ltd, 331 Pinner Road, Harrow, Middlesex, HA1 4HF   *Previous Owner*

HIL6143	Leyland Leopard PSU3C/4R	Plaxton Supreme III	C44F	1976	
HIL8251	Leyland Leopard PSU3C/4R	Plaxton Supreme III	C53F	1976	
HIL4415	Leyland Leopard PSU3E/4R	Plaxton Supreme IV	C44F	1979	
HIL4436	Leyland Leopard PSU5C/4R	Plaxton Supreme IV	C57F	1979	
HIL5953	Leyland Leopard PSU5C/4R	Plaxton Supreme IV	C57F	1979	
HIL3807	Leyland Tiger TRCTL11/3R	Plaxton Paramount 3200	C55F	1983	Premier-Albanian, Watford, 1987
HIL8907	Volvo B10M-61	Plaxton Paramount 3500	C50F	1983	Epsom Coaches, 1992
HIL8984	Volvo B10M-61	Plaxton Paramount 3500	C50F	1983	Epsom Coaches, 1992
A519LPP	Leyland Tiger TRCTL11/3R	Plaxton Paramount 3200	C53F	1983	Smith, Challock, 1996
HIL2173	Leyland Tiger TRCTL11/3R	Plaxton Paramount 3200 II	C55F	1985	Armchair, Brentford, 1986
JIL7308	Volvo B10M-61	Plaxton Paramount 3200 III	C53F	1987	Frames Rickards, Bloomsbury, 1994
JIL7309	Volvo B10M-61	Plaxton Paramount 3200 III	C53F	1987	Frames Rickards, Bloomsbury, 1994
HIL8548	Volvo B10M-61	Plaxton Paramount 3200 III	C53F	1988	Sovereign, 1997
HIL5952	Volvo B10M-60	Plaxton Paramount 3200 III	C53F	1989	Frames Rickards, Bloomsbury, 1995
M590GRY	Toyota Coaster HZB50R	Caetano Optimo III	C21F	1994	

Previous Registrations:-

HIL2173	B403CMC	**HIL5952**	F894SMV	**HIL8251**	NNK811P	**HIL8984**	NGT304Y
HIL3807	KBM103Y	**HIL5953**	GBM126T	**HIL8548**	E358NEG	**JIL7308**	D546KMG
HIL4415	GBM124T	**HIL6143**	NNK810P	**HIL8907**	NGT303Y	**JIL7309**	D547KMG
HIL4436	GBM127T						

Livery:- Jasmine yellow and dark blue.

WESTBUS

Westbus (UK) Ltd, 27a Spring Grove Road, Hounslow, Middlesex, TW3 4BE   *Previous Owner*

YUX611	Volvo B10M-61	Plaxton Supreme V	C50F	1982	Miller, Box, 1996
URU650X	Volvo B10M-56	Plaxton Supreme V Express	C53F	1982	Buddens, Romsey, 1996
WIB7186	Volvo B10M-61	Jonckheere Jubilee P599	C49FT	1987	
WIB7187	Volvo B10M-61	Jonckheere Jubilee P599	C49FT	1987	
WIB7188	Volvo B10M-53	Jonckheere Jubilee P95	CH49/12DT	1987	
WIB7189	Volvo B10M-53	Jonckheere Jubilee P95	CH49/12DT	1987	
WIB8750	Volvo B10M-60	Jonckheere Deauville P599	C49FT	1989	
J361NLM	Toyota Coaster HDB30R	Caetano Optimo II	C18F	1992	Spirit of London, Hounslow, 1995
K508WNR	Volvo B10M-60	Jonckheere Deauville P599	C51FT	1993	
K509WNR	Volvo B10M-60	Jonckheere Deauville P599	C51FT	1993	
M726KJU	Volvo B6	Jonckheere Ascot	C35F	1995	
M727KJU	Volvo B10M-62	Jonckheere Deauville 45	C53F	1995	
N117RJF	Volvo B10M-62	Jonckheere Deauville 45	C51FT	1996	
N118RJF	Volvo B10M-62	Jonckheere Deauville 45	C51FT	1996	
P115HCF	Dennis Javelin SFD731BR3TGJ4	Berkhof Axial	C53F	1997	
P116HCF	Volvo B10M-62	Berkhof Axial	C51FT	1997	
P117HCF	Volvo B10M-62	Berkhof Axial	C51FT	1997	

Previous Registrations:-

J361NLM	A15SOL	**WIB7187**	D102BNV	**WIB7189**	D104BNV	**YUX611**	YDH243X
WIB7186	D101BNV	**WIB7188**	D103BNV	**WIB8750**	F906YNV		

Livery:- Red and cream with black relief.

WEST KINGSDOWN

West Kingsdown Coach Hire Ltd, The Coach Station, London Road, West Kingsdown, Kent, TN15 6AR   *Previous Owner*

KUC228P	Daimler Fleetline CRL6-30	MCW	H44/32F	1976	Hedingham & District, 1997
OJD161R	Leyland Fleetline FE30AGR	Park Royal	H44/32F	1976	A1 Service, Ardrossan, 1997
OJD191R	Leyland Fleetline FE30AGR	MCW	H44/32F	1976	Yellow Buses, Bournemouth, 1995
OUC45R	Leyland Fleetline FE30AGR	MCW	H44/32F	1976	Yellow Buses, Bournemouth, 1995
OJD225R	Leyland Fleetline FE30AGR	MCW	H44/32F	1977	Yellow Buses, Bournemouth, 1995
OJD243R	Leyland Fleetline FE30AGR	MCW	H45/25D	1977	Metrobus, Orpington, 1995
SDA632S	Leyland Fleetline FE30AGR	Park Royal	H43/33F	1977	MTL, Heysham, 1995
581AET	Kassbohrer Setra S215HD	Kassbohrer Tornado	C49FT	1983	Coach Travel, Ightham, 1993
KWV992	Kassbohrer Setra S215HD	Kassbohrer Tornado	C49FT	1987	Boon, Boreham, 1995

E344MLC	Kassbohrer Setra S215HR	Kassbohrer Rational	C53F	1988	Capital, West Drayton, 1996
E345MLC	Kassbohrer Setra S215HR	Kassbohrer Rational	C53F	1988	Capital, West Drayton, 1996
J2WKC	Kassbohrer Setra S215HD	Kassbohrer Tornado	C49FT	1992	Travellers, Hounslow, 1994
M2WKC	Kassbohrer Setra S250	Kassbohrer Special	C48FT	1995	
N2WKC	Kassbohrer Setra S250	Kassbohrer Special	C48FT	1996	
N3WKC	Toyota Coaster HZB50R	Caetano Optimo III	C21F	1996	
P649MKO	Kassbohrer Setra S250	Kassbohrer Special	C48FT	1997	
P773NKE	Kassbohrer Setra S250	Kassbohrer Special	C48FT	1997	

Previous Registrations:-

KWV992	E494EPM, WSU225, E961JHJ	**E344MLC**	3401MW	**J2WKC**	J2TCC
581AET	AMX802Y	**E345MLC**	1068MW		

Livery:- White with turquoise and dark blue flashes.

WEST'S COACHES

West's Coaches Ltd, 198-200 High Road, Woodford Bridge, Essex, IG8 9EF   *Previous Owner*

KGA56Y	Bova EL26/581	Bova Europa	C53F	1982	Crawford, Neilston, 1987
A15BUS	Bova EL28/581	Duple Calypso	C53F	1982	Clements, Nailsea, 1985
A14BUS	Bova EL28/581	Duple Calypso	C53F	1984	Antler, Rugeley, 1988
A10BUS	Volvo B10M-60	Plaxton Paramount 3200 III	C53F	1987	Andrews, Trudoxhill, 1995
A12BUS	DAF SB2305DHS585	Caetano Algarve	C53F	1989	Abbeyways-Hanson, Halifax, 1991
A13BUS	TAZ D3200	TAZ Dubrava	C53F	1989	
A16BUS	Volvo B10M-60	Plaxton Paramount 3500 III	C53F	1989	Fishwick, Leyland, 1992
A18BUS	Volvo B10M-60	Plaxton Paramount 3500 III	C55F	1989	Essex Coachways, Bow, 1994
A19BUS	DAF SB3000DKV601	Caetano Algarve	C49FT	1989	Ace, Mansfield, 1993
H20BUS	Volvo B10M-60	Plaxton Paramount 3500 III	C53F	1991	Camden, Sevenoaks, 1997
A17BUS	DAF SB2305DHS585	Caetano Algarve	C49FT	1992	Browne, East Grinstead, 1996

Previous Registrations:-

A10BUS	D267HFX, XEL55S, D569KJT	**A15BUS**	A321HFP	**A18BUS**	F813TMD
A12BUS	F233RJX	**A16BUS**	F972HGE	**A19BUS**	G949VBC
A13BUS	F788TBC	**A17BUS**	J516LRY	**H20BUS**	H840AHS
A14BUS	B127DHL				

Livery:- White.

WESTWAY

D.J. West, 1 Belmont Road, Belmont, Surrey, SM2 6DW   *Previous Owner*

B111CCS	Volvo B10M-61	Jonckheere Jubilee P599	C53F	1985	Jenkins, Skewen, 1990
UVF47	Volvo B10M-53	Jonckheere Jubilee P95	CH49/12DT	1987	Westbus, Hounslow, 1997
F703COA	Volvo B10M-53	Plaxton Paramount 4000 III RS	CH53/12DT	1989	Flights, Birmingham, 1995
F981HGE	Volvo B10M-60	Plaxton Paramount 3500 III	C53F	1989	Fuggles, Benenden, 1994
KIB545	Volvo B10M-60	Berkhof Excellence 2000	C49FT	1990	The Kings Ferry, Gillingham, 1995
G758ELV	Volvo B10M-60	Van Hool Alizee H	C53F	1990	Warrington, 1995
G227GEL	Mercedes-Benz 609D	Reeve Burgess Beaver	C23F	1990	Bicknell, Godalming, 1996
LIB378	Volvo B10M-53	Van Hool Alizee SH	C49FT	1990	Classic, Annfield Plain, 1996
L914NWW	Volvo B10M-60	Van Hool Alizee	C48FT	1994	Putt, Morden,1997
N991BWJ	Volvo B10M-62	Van Hool Alizee HE	C49FT	1996	

Previous Registrations:- **KIB545**   G416WPA   **LIB378**   G500CVC   **UVF47**   D105BNV, WIB7190

Livery:- Blue with orange relief.

WINGS/ALLIED

Wings Luxury Travel Ltd, 126-127 Waterloo Road, Uxbridge, Middlesex, UB8 2QZ
Allied Coachlines Ltd, 126-127 Waterloo Road, Uxbridge, Middlesex, UB8 2QZ   *Previous Owner*

Wings Fleet

B666OVU	Ford Transit	Mellor	C16F	1984	Hooper, Harrow Weald, 1996
C633XVU	Ford Transit	Mellor	C16F	1986	Cooke-Willing, Feltham, 1996
D642ELH	Ford Transit	Ford	M8	1987	MCH, Uxbridge, 1996
WLT731	Ford Transit	Dormobile	C16F	1991	Bailey, Iver, 1997
WLT746	Mercedes-Benz 814D	Optare StarRider	C29F	1993	
WET590	Mercedes-Benz 814D	Optare StarRider	C20FT	1994	
WET880	Mercedes-Benz 814D	Optare StarRider	C20FT	1994	
WLT852	Mercedes-Benz 814D	Optare StarRider	C29F	1994	
WLT732	Mercedes-Benz 814D	Optare StarRider	C29F	1994	
WET476	Kassbohrer Setra S210H	Kassbohrer Optimal	C24FT	1995	
WET725	Kassbohrer Setra S210H	Kassbohrer Optimal	C24F	1995	
WLT289	Ford Transit	Mellor	M16	1995	
WLT987	Ford Transit	Mellor	M16	1995	
WET342	Mercedes-Benz 814D	Robin Hood RH2000	C16FT	1996	
WET859	Mercedes-Benz 814D	Robin Hood RH2000	C16FT	1996	
P478NKM	Mercedes-Benz 814D	Robin Hood RH2000	C25F	1997	

Allied Fleet

N784ORY	Dennis Javelin 12SDA2134	Caetano Algarve II	C48FT	1995	
N786SJU	Dennis Javelin 12SDA2134	Caetano Algarve III	C51FT	1996	
N787SJU	Dennis Javelin 12SDA2134	Caetano Algarve III	C51FT	1996	
N952SPD	Dennis Javelin 12SDA2144	Auwaerter Transliner	C49FT	1995	Dennis demonstrator, 1996
N861RFU	Kassbohrer Setra S250	Kassbohrer Special	C48FT	1996	
N862RFU	Kassbohrer Setra S250	Kassbohrer Special	C48FT	1996	
P567VEE	Kassbohrer Setra S250	Kassbohrer Special	C48FT	1997	
P568VEE	Kassbohrer Setra S250	Kassbohrer Special	C48FT	1997	

Previous Registrations:-

WET342	N257CKR	**WET725**	M413MPD	**WLT289**	M910AMA, WLT987	**WLT746**	L835MWT
WET476	M412MPD	**WET859**	N256CKR	**WLT731**	H844SWF	**WLT852**	M928TYG
WET590	L860DPK	**WET880**	L861DPK	**WLT732**	M929TYG	**WLT987**	M901AMA

Liveries:- Wings :- White with red, orange and yellow relief.
Allied :- White with blue relief.

Special Liveries:- Eurolines (White with red and blue fleetnames) :- N862RFU, P567VEE, P568VEE.
Visitors Sightseeing (White with red, yellow and black fleetnames) :- N784ORY

LEN WRIGHT

Len Wright Band Services Ltd, 9 Elton Way, Watford, Hertfordshire, WD2 8HH   *Previous Owner*

WSV505	Volvo B10M-61	Van Hool Astral	C6/6DT	1984	Cantabrica, Watford, 1991
E689NNH	Scania K112CRS	Jonckheere Jubilee P599	C10FT	1988	Cantabrica, Watford, 1991
E690NNH	Scania K112CRS	Jonckheere Jubilee P599	C10FT	1988	Cantabrica, Watford, 1991
F959RNV	Volvo B10M-61	Jonckheere Jubilee P599	C10FT	1988	Cantabrica, Watford, 1991
F68SMC	Volvo B10M-53	Van Hool Astral 3	CH8/7FT	1988	Cantabrica, Watford, 1991
G95VMM	Volvo B10M-50	Van Hool Astral 3	CH8/7FT	1989	Cantabrica, Watford, 1991
G96VMM	Volvo B10M-50	Van Hool Astral 3	CH8/7FT	1989	Cantabrica, Watford, 1991
K2LWB	Scania K113CRB	Plaxton Excalibur	C10FT	1993	
L3LWB	Volvo B12R	Plaxton Prestige 370	C10FT	1994	
N4LWB	Scania K113TRB	Irizar Century 12.37	C10FT	1996	
N5LWB	Scania K113TRB	Irizar Century 12.37	C10FT	1996	

Note:- L3LWB is a left hand drive vehicle

The Len Wright fleet is used exclusively as mobile hotels on tour with bands and other show business companies, especially abroad. All coaches are fitted with a small number of seats as well as bunks as follows:-

10 bunks:- E689NNH, E690NNH, F959RNV, K2LWB, L3LWB, N4LWB, N5LWB
12 bunks:- WSV505
15 bunks:- F68SMC, G95VMM, G96VMM

Named Vehicles:- F68SMC   Gold II   G95VMM   Gold III   G96VMM   Gold IV

Previous Registration:- **WSV505**   A59OTA

Livery:- Metallic grey and red.

The lists in this edition were finalised on 1st September 1997